A
Travel Guide
Through Children's
Literature

Hope Blecher-Sass
Catherine Waddington
Merry Law

Alleyside Press®

Fort Atkinson, Wisconsin

Acknowledgments

As a mother, wife, educator and community volunteer, I would not have been able to write this book without the many people who worked behind the scenes. Thank you to our sitters, Claire Brown, Nicole Harder, Jennifer Eisenberg, Jennifer and Jaclyn Genega, and Emmery Schultz for the hours they spent watching Loren and Colin so that I could work and get to the post office. Thank you to Loren, CJ and my husband Raymond for their cooperation and patience. Thank you to Rose McGrath and Susan Moskal of Barnes and Noble Booksellers, Clark, NJ for helping me to locate the books. Thanks to the staff of the Clark Library for your assistance with reference questions and for re-shelving many books. Tracy Watt and Merry Law, thank you for all of your computer assistance. Thank you to the publisher and editor who saw this and got it into your hands. Also, for their continued words of support and guidance, thank you to Dr. Maurice Elias, and my parents, Louis and Helen Blecher. A final thank you to the man who unknowingly started me on this project, Dr. Anthony Colella. To all, what can I say but let me know if I can ever help you.
Hope Blecher-Sass

I would like to thank Hope Blecher-Sass for her suggestion to collaborate on this project. It allowed me to research answers to questions I have always had about my favorite books. I appreciate my co-authors' support and patience while working on this project, and thank the editor and publisher for bringing this information to publication. **Cathy Waddington**

Thanks to my co-authors for re-awakening me to the joys of children's literature, to Wayne for his patience and advice as I worked on this project, and to our editor and publisher for making this book a reality.
Merry Law

Published by **Alleyside Press**, an imprint of Highsmith Press
Highsmith Press
W5527 Highway 106
P.O. Box 800
Fort Atkinson, Wisconsin 53538-0800
1-800-558-2110

© Hope Blecher-Sass, Catherine Waddington, Merry Law, 2001
Cover design: Debra Neu Sletten

The paper used in this publication meets the minimum requirements of American National Standard for Information Science — Permanence of Paper for Printed Library Material. ANSI/NISO Z39.48-1992.

Library of Congress Cataloging-in-Publication Data
Blecher-Sass, Hope, 1962-
  A travel guide through children's literature / Hope Blecher-Sass,
Catherine Waddington, Merry Law.
      p. cm.
Includes bibliographical references and index.
  ISBN 1-57950-074-9 (alk. paper)
  1. Children–Books and reading–United States. 2. Activity programs
in education. 3. Interdisciplinary approach in education. 4. Geography
in literature. 5. Children's literature–Bibliography. I. Waddington,
Catherine, 1963- II. Law, Merry, 1949- III. Title.
   Z1037.A1 B5825 2001
   028.5'5'0973–dc21
                                    2001004895

Contents

Introduction

Reading is a skill that allows children to succeed in school and in life. Librarians, media specialists and teachers can encourage children's love for reading by sharing literature with them. Reading aloud with children provides an insight into the child's way of seeing the world through their emotional reactions, intellectual comments and reflections on the stories' events. Stories create avenues for sharing desires, goals, fears and dreams. Another read-aloud benefit to children is the opportunity for them to hear the words and create an image in their minds. Hearing language is an important part of phonemic awareness and mastery of sounds and syllables. Through reading aloud, the educator is helping the children to construct meaning for the story as well as for the spoken words.

Role-modeling

Within the class or the library, the teacher or librarian is the role model who instills a passion for reading, preparing the children to become responsible readers who will be able to read independently and silently for meaning. By reading to and with children, educators give the subtle message that reading and writing are useful and meaningful. Educators can also help the children to make connections between the stories and the world outside so that they can use and apply their skills and knowledge to real-life situations. During storytime, the educator should also apply knowledge of the various learning styles, presentation modes and language abilities, in order to better foster the development of connections.

Making Connections

Teachers and librarians are in a position to assist children with making connections between written words, stories and real life. There are choices that reflect children's areas of interest and that correspond with curriculum themes. The titles can be used in conjunction with selections that appear in the Language Arts series of the teacher's school district.

Book Selection

We selected books for this guide that reflect a variety of classroom themes and literary genres. Therefore, this book is useful to teachers, librarians and parents—children's first teachers. The selections support those who are working to foster an appreciation for the richness of literature while building the foundation of literacy. You may chose titles from here that also reflect the interests of the students and curriculum themes. This will facilitate the blending of prior experiences and knowledge with the benefits gained through exposure to the stories.

Other selection criteria include: our enjoyment of reading these books; the experiences we've had as parents and educators; inclusion of a range of locations and topics—there should be something for each reader's taste; and award honors (see Appendix B for a complete listing of award books).

Embarking on a Journey

Whichever books you select to read and wherever you find them, we hope this guide inspires you to explore the stories and to embark on a journey between and beyond the pages of the book. You are opening up pathways and guiding students on a course that will broaden their horizons. That is an important task with many implications. Every time you read with a child you are helping them to understand the power of the written and the spoken words. When nurtured, that power can support and influence the literacy of generations.

How to Use This Book

General Information

Please read any story yourself before reading it to an audience at home or at school to avoid unpleasant surprises. While the information contained in this book is accurate at the time it was written, Internet sites, telephone numbers and even addresses can change. Before making plans, please double check that the information remains accurate. While we have checked websites and contact information, inclusion in this book does not imply endorsement by the authors of the businesses or locations.

Read-aloud Ages

The read-aloud ages are suggested age ranges of children who will enjoy listening to the stories. They are in no manner definitive, so you have the freedom to choose books that you like and think the children or students will enjoy. In some instances, the age range reflects the theme and language of the story. The older ages usually mean the story's theme or content is for upper elementary to middle school students. Some stories appeal to a broad range of ages and re-visiting a familiar story at a later age may bring new or deeper understanding to the material it contains.

Maps and Geography

A map, globe or atlas is useful when reading these books. In the classroom, a large map that can be displayed on a wall for the entire school year is preferable. Whether you are in a school, library or at home as you read the books and take the real or imaginary trips, you can mark the locations on the map or list them on a chart. Begin by locating your state and town on the map. To encourage the use of maps and of map skills, have children draw a map of their neighborhood, a map of the school or a map of their bedroom. These maps can be used as prompts for oral or written stories. (See also the reproducible U.S. and world maps at the back of this guide.)

A *Travel Guide Through Children's Literature* is a useful resource for teachers and librarians who are planning geography lessons. (National Geography Awareness Week occurs during the middle of November.) Teachers and librarians can select a book, read with the children and then locate the places using different types of maps, such as a topographical or geophysical map. Have participants locate where they live now and where the sites in the book are located. Trace the route with a string. If you took that journey today, what would you see?

You might want to have older students participate in National Geographic's Geography Bee. Information can be found at www.nationalgeographic.com/geographybee. Younger children may try to visit 100 places by the 100th day of school. You can also use "speaking" maps such as the one in LeapPad's touch-interactive books. With the LeapPad book, someone can touch a place on the US map and be told the name of the state, the capital and how far it is from a second state selected.

Writing, Drawing and Music

Children can be encouraged to keep a journal to record the books and where they have visited, either in real visits or through Internet visits. To encourage writing and to explore diverse locations and cultures, they can have pen and paper or on-line pen pals. Children who enjoy drawing or painting can make a travel poster advertising a book and the locales. Those who are musical could learn and perform the song of a particular state or a song related to other locales in a book. Plan a performance or assembly for an audience of peers and parents. Students' learning will shine through during the show. You can also foster a community connection by inviting a group to perform at the school or library. You could even arrange for the group's spokesperson to talk with the students ahead of time and include a mention of the project in their presentation. The children will be thrilled when the guests know what's happening in their classroom or library.

Interdisciplinary Ideas

Research has shown that skills do not develop in isolation. Learners of all ages can transfer knowledge from one area to another and use it in different contexts. Using an interdisciplinary approach to education helps to promote the use of skills across the curriculum. This guide helps educators to follow an interdisciplinary approach when planning and implementing units of study. A teacher can combine a history lesson with reading skills, map skills, math skills and writing skills. Likewise, a teacher can start with the reading lesson and bring in computer and technology skills, map skills and a geography or history lesson. Below are two sample units that illustrate how an educator could develop a theme by using the information in this book. This book can be a useful resource for teachers who want to devise interdisciplinary curriculum models.

Sample 1

History as the starting point for students in grades 4–5 studying the Revolutionary War period:

Reading Skills: Suggested titles are *American Girl*, Felicity series; *And Then What Happened Paul Revere?*; *Ben and Me, An Astonishing Life of Benjamin Franklin as Written by His Good Mouse Amos*; *Paul Revere's Ride* and *Johnny Tremain*. Have students compare and contrast all the characters.

Computer and Technology Skills: Using the information provided about these titles, have students go to some of the suggested websites to find places to visit. Take a virtual tour of at least one site.

Map Skills: Give students a map of the United States and have them plot the locations found during the virtual tour using the computer on the map. Have a discussion of why all these stories are located only on the East Coast of the U.S.

Math Skills: Given the scale on a map, have students calculate mileage between Ben Franklin's House and Felicity's house, Ben Franklin's house and Paul Revere's house Ben Franklin's and Johnny Tremain's houses. Who lives closest to Ben Franklin? Who lives farthest away from Ben Franklin? Who lives closest to each other?

Writing Skills: Have students write a description of a party where Ben Franklin, Felicity, Paul Revere and Johnny Tremain were present. What would they say to one another? What would they wear? What would they eat? Where would the party be held?

Sample 2

Reading as the starting point for students in grades 1–2.

Reading Skills: *Make Way for Ducklings* is the suggested reading. Discuss the reason Mrs. Mallard was so fussy about choosing where to hatch her ducklings.

Computer and Technology Skills: Visit the Boston website and view the actual location of Mr. and Mrs. Mallard's adventure.

Map Skills: Using a big U.S. map, help students to find Boston and their own town. Discuss whether Boston is north, south, east or west of their town.

Science Skills: Study ducks and their habits and habitats. Have students decide if the Mallards chose a site that most ducks would choose to have ducklings. Discuss whether Mrs. Mallard is like other duck mothers.

Writing Skills: Have students choose to be one of the ducklings. Have them draw a picture of how they would swim in the Public Garden and maybe an adventure they might have there. After they illustrate, have students write about their picture.

Community or Home Cooperation with the School or Library

These activities and ideas foster cooperation between the teacher or librarian and the home or community to engage children in relating information in books to the world around them. Some activities may be more appropriate for schools or for libraries. They are presented to suggest some of the many ways that the books in *A Travel Guide Through Children's Literature* can be used.

Having Guests: Who has been to _____ ?

Send out a letter to parents and guardians or post a notice in the library with the intention of finding a person who has visited the locale of a story. This is an opportunity for parents and community members to become guests in the classroom or the children's group. On a chart, brainstorm with the children regarding what they learned about this location from reading the book. List the locations and descriptions. The guest can help the children contrast the descriptions in the book with what the place is really like.

Visit From an Author or Illustrator

You might want to invite a local author or illustrator to come and meet with the children to explain the work involved in putting a book together. Authors may also appear at local bookstores to read from their works. If an author is appearing in the area, you may be able to arrange a visit to the school or library before the author arrives by writing to the publisher.

Museums

After reading a book, do a bit of research through the Internet or through the yellow pages of a phone book to locate a local history museum or historical society. Often members do outreach programs to schools or libraries. Perhaps a field trip can be arranged to the museum or society. If the story had a particular time setting, often the members can dress to reflect the clothing of the time. Children really enjoy seeing this. It is a step back in time and helps them picture what it was like then.

Recipes

Some of the stories include recipes. Cooking incorporates many curriculum components. Bring the book to life by really making the item in the book. This is a good opportunity to invite parents in to assist with an activity. If you wait until you have five or six dishes, you can have a Storybook Recipe Program, where the families read together sections of the books and eat the foods. An international element can be added by using stories from other countries. (See **Animals and Food** on p. 11.)

School and Home Preparations

Visitors and Public Relations

Children may be interested in having people from the locations in a book visit them. Parents, guardians and other relatives may be from the locations in the books you are reading. Discuss the potential project with parents and guardians and explain how it is related to what their child is doing. Let them know you are interested in guests and would like their assistance with some aspects of the project.

When there is a guest, it may be of interest to a broader audience than the children. Invite parents and families. Inform visitors when they are invited that there may be outside guests and that they may be photographed or videotaped so that they can dress accordingly.

Contact the local newspapers and radio stations. This is an opportunity to share with the community a positive story about the school or library in your town. The lead time for coverage by a photographer and reporter may be three weeks, so call or fax as soon as you are organized for the event. You should also recheck the week prior to remind the editor and reconfirm the coverage of your event. Some media directors will not send a reporter or photographer but will welcome your submission of a story, photograph and videotape. Send copies, not originals, because the items are rarely returned. You can submit these to a local newspaper, make copies of them and have the video playing for a special night event.

Know your school's or library's policy about photographing the children. If necessary send home a note informing the adults about the event and have a tear-off so that an okay or not can be received from each child. Some schools do this in the beginning of the year in a general letter that covers potential recordings. Some parents will not want a child to be recorded. In that case, place the child in the group, but to the side. Be aware of that child's position and abide by the parents' wishes.

Animals and Food

Peanut and milk allergies are a concern in schools. Some children and adults may also have animal allergies. Although this information should be known to the school nurse, if animals or food are involved, ask the children about allergies. Verify the information with the school nurse or a parent or guardian. Teachers and librarians should send home a notification to parents and guardians before the event. The notice should have a tear-off return portion requesting a list of allergies to food or animals. A check box for "no known allergies" should be included so that each student returns a notice.

Sample School-Home Notices

Sample for Photographs and Videotapes

Dear Parents/Guardians,

During the school year, the students are involved in many programs and assemblies. Some of these are covered by the media for newspaper and radio reports. This is done to spread the good news about what is happening in our school.

We would appreciate your cooperation in signing the form and returning it to the homeroom teacher by _____. Thank you for helping us to promote our educational programs.

(date)

Sincerely,

_____
(teacher's name)

_____
(principal's name)

- -

To promote and encourage the public to support the school's educational programs, I consent to the use by the school of the name, photograph, video, artwork or picture of my child. I release the school from any liability that should occur.

Child's name (print) _____

Homeroom teacher (print) _____

Parent/Guardian's name (print) _____

Parent/Guardian's signature _____

Date _____

Dear Parents/Guardians,

As part of the educational experience your child will have at our school, there will be assembly programs. Some of these programs might include opportunities to taste foods and to see or pet small animals. Therefore, for the safety of the child, we need to know about any allergies.

Please complete this form and return it to the homeroom teacher by
_____.
      (date)

Sincerely,

_____

(teacher's name)

_____

(principal's name)

- -

Check one:

_____ My child has allergies. Please list all known allergies in the space below.

_____

_____

_____ My child has no known allergies.

Child's name (print) _____

Homeroom teacher (print) _____

Parent/Guardian's name (print) _____

Parent/Guardian's signature _____

Date _____

Adaptable Activities

Various activities can be done in the class, library or home in order to extend a book beyond its covers. These activities can be customized for the specific stories and audience. Use this list as a starting point, and create other games that are appropriate for your situation. Although we have listed the activities under headings such as "Art & Music" and "Geography & History," many of these activities are interdisciplinary—incorporating writing, drawing, geography and comprehension skills.

Art and Music

Songs

At a loss for words? Don't worry—there is a site for the words to songs at Kididdles (www.kididdles.com). You will find the titles and words to hundreds of songs, many of which include the names of cities and states. Use this as an opportunity to write a song in which the children would include the names of the characters, the names of the places or the events. After you have enough and the children are fluent in the songs, put on a Singing Travel Guide Concert for the parents. This is a good opportunity to ask for the music teacher's cooperation or to invite a local musician to provide assistance, with writing, performing or contributing musical accompaniment.

Story Mobiles

You will need yarn or string; pieces of blank paper at least 2" to a side in the shapes of squares, circles or triangles; crayons; pencils; and a hanger or thin wooden dowel. The children can illustrate their favorite characters or favorite scenes from the story on the paper shapes. Tie the illustrations onto the dowel or hanger and suspend these by hooks or suction cups from the ceilings or walls. These can be used as story retelling aides or to continue a story into the future.

Flip Books

Flip books are simple animations that the children can create themselves. You will need paper fasteners or a stapler; pencils; crayons; and 7–10 paper rectangles per child, measuring about 2x4". On their desks or tables, the students put the papers in a row. Each chooses a sequence of actions or a character to be illustrated. Simple illustrations are best. On the lower third of the first paper, illustrate one action or character. Then move to the next paper and draw the next action or movement by the character. Continue drawing on each paper with a slight change in the character or action. Fasten the papers together in order at the top. Hold the book at the top by the fastened end. Use your other hand to fan or flip the pages and watch what happens. The still sequence appears to be moving.

Shoebox Diorama

Use an empty shoebox to create a scene from the story. We have seen these scenes moved from the inside of the box to the top, depending upon the scene to be created such as a room versus a landscape. Pasting pictures for the scene to the inside of the lid may be easier for younger children than trying to place the picture inside the box.

Footsteps

The title of this project is, "We Walked To…." You will need a map of your town, manila paper, crayons and yarn or string. On manila paper, have the students trace each other's feet. You can do this with shoes or sneakers on, just check the soles for gum or dirt first. Put the name of each child on a slip of paper or a popsicle stick. Before you read a story, choose a child's stick or name card. That child decorates his footprint to show something about the story. It could be the characters, the locations or a favorite scene. Using yarn, glue one end to the location of your school on the town map and the other end to the footprint. Tape this along the perimeter of the map. A variation is to tape the footsteps along the perimeter of the walls of the class-room or the hallways of the school or around the library.

Travel Brochure

Look at travel brochures for examples of what to include in the layout and the content. Have students create a brochure for the story. This is a time for cooperative activities between the children who are good planners, those who are artistic and those who enjoy writing.

Nesting Dolls

This requires non-breakable cups of different sizes. The nesting dolls are created by having each cup represent a character. The largest cup would be the tallest character. Then the next cup is for the next size character, working your way to the smallest character being the smallest cup. The people are created on the cups by either drawing directly onto the cup or by making the figure on paper, then cutting and gluing it onto the cup. The children then put the smallest figure into the smaller figure, into the small figure, into the medium figure into the big figure and finally into the biggest figure so that when you look, all you see is the biggest figure and the others are inside of it.

Paper Plate Crowns

For this project, you need one white paper plate for each child. You will need to show them how to make this, by providing both visual and oral directions. Draw the outline of a figure in the center of the plate touching the rim on one side. Essentially, you are creating a stencil on the center of the plate and cutting out the background leaving the figure attached to the plate's rim on one side. Fold the edge of the figure to stand the stencil upright above the rim of the plate. The plate's rim becomes the brim of a crown that the child can wear with the figure standing against the child's forehead.

Photo Journals

Using illustrations, photographs and picture postcards, create a photo journal for the location of the story. Use this book to find stories that correspond to places where the children have lived or visited. Have those children provide the captions for the pictures.

Paper Doll Characters

Both boys and girls enjoy this activity. Design or find a template for a basic paper doll figure. Have the children use the template to recreate one of the story figures. With older children and with books that have few illustrations, they can design the characters to reflect the descriptions in the story. This is good for a lesson about adjectives and descriptive words such as colors. Such materials as pieces of fabric, assorted buttons, yarn scraps and such can add to the realism of the dolls. Let the children use these as props to retell the story, to tell an incident from their character's perspective or to create dialog for a situation that they would want to change if they could rewrite the story. For some children, it helps them to manipulate the dolls if a popsicle stick is attached to the back, or if a cardboard stand is made. This is simple to do by just cutting a strip of cardboard and folding it in half. Towards each end, cut a slit. Slip the paper doll into the slits and it will stand up.

Games

Puzzlemaker.com http://puzzlemaker.school.discovery.com

On this website you can custom design mazes and word puzzles and adjust the degree of difficulty. As an added bonus, the answer is also available. The puzzle and the solution can be printed out directly from the site. Your list of words can include the words in the title, the locations, the names of the characters or any other vocabulary you may choose.

Puzzles: Fitting the Pieces Together

There are companies that sell blank puzzles. Essentially these are pieces of cardboard with no pictures on them. The students draw the picture, color it and then separate the pieces and the child has made a puzzle. Another way to do this project is to use the thin cardboard that often comes with shirts that have been laundered and put into boxes. The children should first make their illustration and then cut it into the puzzle shapes. Have them turn the pieces over and print their initials on each piece. The pieces are then put into a baggie that has been labeled with the maker's name. This way, if a piece falls onto the floor, it can be returned to the correct bag. Children can put each other's puzzles together, trying to guess which story the puzzle depicts.

Fortune Tellers

Paper "fortune tellers" are another fun way for children to create a game with the locations mentioned in the books.* Start with a 9" or larger square piece of paper. Fold the four corners into the middle and firmly crease the folds. Flip this over and fold the four new corners created by the first folds into the middle. Again, firmly crease the folds. Fold it in half so that you see two squares. Fold it in half again so you have one square. Gently let it open a little bit. Put your forefinger and thumb of each hand into the open bottoms of the squares. Now, bring the fingers to meet so the paper looks a bit like a closed blossom. Then move your fingers out to make the paper pocket close.

Now label the fortune teller. The four outside squares can be labeled with the titles of books or the names of states. For example, print the word "Ping" on one square. Open the fortune teller to look at the two folded triangles that are on the backside of the square. On the left triangle print the word "places" and on the right print the word "characters." Lift up the left triangle and under "places" print the sentence "You will go to the Yangtze River." Under the right triangle, print the sentence "You will visit Ping and say la-la-la-la." Continue labeling the outer squares with book titles, lifting and labeling the triangles until all are filled with a new fact for the children on the innermost side. Experiment and enjoy your travel fortunes.

Klutz Products has a book of these patterns. Some children may call these "cootie catchers."

Clue

Each child, or small group of children, thinks of a story, setting, character or title. Fold a piece of paper in half from top to bottom. On the front, each child or group writes three clues describing the story, setting, character or title. The fourth sentence is a question such as "Who am I?," "Where am I?" or "Which title am I?" Then inside, write or illustrate the item that matches the clues. For example, if you were giving clues for Madeline, you could write, "I live in Paris," "I live with 11 other girls," "I live in a house that is covered with vines," "Who am I?" The answer is "Madeline" and inside the student might have spelled the word Madeline or drawn a picture of her. Each child or group takes a turn asking the question while the other children guess the answer.

Scavenger Hunts

Map, writing and comprehension skills can be incorporated into scavenger hunts. With the children, choose a book based on its location. Use the Location Index on page 83 to check for books in your state or choose a location related to the curriculum. (These scavenger hunts can be real or imaginary.) Make a list of clues and follow the path to the "treasure," which can be an item in the book or the home of a character. Help the children create a map that includes the area of the hunt with features that correspond to possible clues. Parents can be included in this educational adventure, too. They can help create the clues or the children can do the clues and invite the parents to search for the answers in the book.

Physically Active Play

What's On My Back?

In this activity, the participants have to find the two items that go together. The pairs can be identical matches, such as pictures or words, or two items that "go" together, such as a title and main character. On two separate pieces of paper, no bigger than a 5x7", the children, teacher or librarian prints, draws or glues the matching pictures and words. Have the children stand in a line and then come to you one by one. The child turns around, and onto his or her back, you tape a flash card. The child sits in a circle or returns to his or her seat. When all of the cards are taped, the children get up and find their partners. They ask their peers, "What's on my back?" and then listen to the answers. This can be done with odd or even numbers of children by taping two cards onto someone's back. The cards can be used multiple times.

Jump Rope Rhyme

Do you remember the jump rope rhyme, "A my name is Alice and I come from Alabama and I eat apples"? For this activity, you will need two lists, one for names and the other for locations. On the left side of the chart, going down in a column, list the capital letters of the alphabet. For each book, list the names of the characters next to the corresponding capital letter. Do the same for the names of the locations mentioned in each book in another column. For example, after reading *Madeline*, next to "M" you would print "Madeline" and next to "P" you would print "Paris." After you have a name and a location for the same capital letter, you are ready to jump. While jump roping, the students repeat the verse using the poster as a visual aid. A sample completed line would be, "C my name is Carrie and I come from Canada and I eat carrots." (Carrie is a character in the Laura Ingall Wilder's *Little House* series and Canada is the location for *Journey to Freedom*.) This is an educational opportunity to cooperate with the physical education teacher. Jump roping is a skill practiced towards the end of first grade and in second grade. Combining reading, writing, rhymes and jump roping is cross-curriculum learning in action.

Geography and History

Timeline

Fasten pieces of paper together to create a group time line of a number of stories. Begin with your favorite selection. Write the title, time period of the story and location. Children can provide illustrations if you like. Then when you read the next book, repeat the above activity and tape the new selection either to the right or left of the first one, depending upon whether the time is before or after the original choice. Add on more entries as you read more books. Because the sequences may change as time periods for new books are added, do not glue the pieces together, but use tape or brad fasteners.

Geography

The National Geographic Society's magazines, books and website provide a wealth of information. Use AAA to your advantage, too. LeapPad, an electronic teaching tool has a geography section that helps in learning the names of the states, the capitals and the distances between two locations. This is a good time to introduce maps and map measurements to compute the distances between locations. *Where in the World is Carmen San Diego* is a television show, a website and a game that incorporates travel.

Farmer's Almanac

There is a wealth of information in the *Old Farmer's Almanac*. Use back issues to learn more about the particular year and place that relates to the book you have read. Gather information from the children to "predict" the events of the next month in your community. Predictions can be worked into lesson plans around Ground Hog's Day, so have fun with it. The *Old Farmer's Almanac* has an interesting website at www.almanac.com, although they offer fewer predictions on-line.

Vacation Planner

Have the children become travel agents for themselves or one another. Use a map to find a location or locations to take a real or imaginary vacation. After identifying locations, use this book to find literature that corresponds to the sites the vacation will visit or be near. Read one or more of the books and create postcards to "send" to the each other. (See **Postcards** below.) Actually or virtually visit the vacation site(s). Write a travel brochure for the location. (See **Travel Brochure** on p.15.)

Book Maps

Using a blank map of the U.S. or the world, color a state or country as you read a story that takes place there (see the reproducible maps at the back of this guide). Add pictures of items or images from the story. This activity is particularly good for stories that mention a large number of states or countries, such as *This Land Is Your Land, The Little Prince* or *Bound for Oregon.*

State Quarters

Obtain an empty quarter collection map. The state quarters are being released a few each year. With the permission of the principal, ask students to look for the quarters that correspond to the states on the map. This is also a time to learn about the order in which the colonies and territories became what are now our 50 United States of America. You could extend this to money activities. This is also the appropriate time to invite a coin collector to the class. Students could also take a trip, either in person or via books, videos and the Internet, to the Federal Mint to learn the coin making process. Studying coins or the states can also help them to learn the names of some of our past presidents.

Postcards

Using a large U.S. or world map, thin yarn, tape and postcards, you can plot the places that the children have visited. Tape the map to a wall. Ask the children, staff and their families to look for a postcard that corresponds to the location. Attach one end of the yarn to the location on the map. Attach the other end to the back of the postcard and tape this along the perimeter of the map. You can also combine this with writing letters or sending e-mails. You can write to the local Chamber of Commerce of the town and ask them to send you a postcard. You can contact, via mail or e-mail, the post office in the town, too. The Postmaster can send you a card with the postmark. Several classes around the country have had success with this.

Language and Writing

Movie and Book Critics

If the book has been made into a movie, view the video after you have read the book. Does the video stick to the story? What was changed? Why might those changes have been made? Which did you prefer, the book or the video, and why? Sometimes, a friendly editor will permit you to run an article with the children's reviews. This is worth pursuing; it is a way to get your good efforts out into the community and parents frequently love to see their child's name in print. Books and movies are good opportunities for home-school connections. In a letter to the parents, inform them that the children will be learning about critiques. In the process of becoming critics, their writings will be submitted to a local newspaper, whose editor might select the items for publication. Their children will experience the thrill of being published!

Foreign Languages

Does the book take place in a foreign location? Which language is spoken there? Does someone in the group know that language? Does a community member know that language? Learn how to say a few words or sentences such as "Hello," "How are you?" and "Have a nice day." Learn to count from 1 to 10, to say the days of the week or the names of objects important in the story in the second language. You might also find that the book was written in another language or has been translated into other languages. Obtain a copy in another language and share it with the children. A guest who speaks that language can be invited to read passages out loud. There are many tapes, both audio and video, available with kid's songs sung in languages other than English. A fun teaching game to play is Simon Says. Do it a few times in English and then in another language. You'll see lots of smiles.

Letters to Authors and Illustrators

Have you really enjoyed a particular book? Are there illustrations that really catch your eye? Use those to prompt the children to write letters to the author or illustrator. Many authors and illustrators have websites that can be found by doing a search. You can also send mail to the publisher who will forward it to the authors. The publishing information is usually found on the second or third page of the book with the copyright information. To protect the privacy of the children, you can use the school's or library's address as the return address. Send the letters with a cover letter explaining that this was a class project.

Virtual Field Trips

It would be ideal if we could visit all of the places referred to in the books. However, since that is not practical, use the Internet as your travel tool. Many of the towns, museums and buildings offer virtual tours through their websites. Have children keep a written journal of what you learn during your virtual travel as a travel log. Some suggestions for using the Internet with children are offered in the next chapter, "Visiting the Site: Virtual and Real."

Word Finds

Word finds are a great educational tool. Having tried to make these from scratch, there is now an easier way. With the assistance of Puzzelmaker at http://puzzlemaker. school.discovery.com, an adult or the child can type in the vocabulary words and the site will provide the word find and solution. Puzzlemaker has become part of Discovery (www.discovery.com), so there are other educational tools available, as well on School Discovery (http://school.discovery.com).

The Story Continues

This activity lets the children be authors and illustrators. Ask children, "Have you ever read a story and not wanted it to end? Many readers feel this way." Let the children explore the possibilities by adding onto the story. If they could turn the page and read more of the story or see another illustration, what would appear? Let them write and draw the next page. Compile this into an epilogue and read it out loud to the group. You could also make a photocopy of it and send it to the author and illustrator of the book. Often, you will receive an acknowledgment and perhaps you will have provided material for another book.

Alphabetical Order

The children can arrange the words in the title in alphabetical order. As more and more books are read, the difficulty of the alphabetizing increases. You can adjust that according to the age and abilities of the students, using one title or many titles

Letters Make Words

This is fun to do with letter flashcards or letter blocks. On a sentence strip or a long piece of paper, print the title of a book using lower case letters. The children rearrange the letters to spell other words. Caution: Depending upon the ages and street-smarts of the children, you will want to monitor for unacceptable or slang words. For example, with the title *Make Way for Ducklings*, you can form the words luck, go, from and may. (There is also the potential to have letter combinations that would be offensive.)

Visiting the Site
Virtual and Real

Using the Internet with Children

Internet literacy is becoming an important skill. The ability to use the Internet to search for information, to move through the World Wide Web and to evaluate the content will be a skill children need as they move on in life.

Children need to be taught the skills to locate and critically review information on the Internet. Since anyone can publish a Web page, unlike traditional print information sources, the need for critical thinking and the ability to analyze the information found is important. The fundamentals of plagiarism, copyright and intellectual property rights need to be taught to younger children and reinforced with older ones, emphasizing the different context of the Web.

Among the many educational resources on the Internet, the following sites will provide a starting place for teachers, librarians and parents:

- *Yahooligans Teacher's Guide* (www.yahooligans.com/tg). Sponsored by Yahoo!, this site has information on teaching Internet literacy and for reviewing and evaluating sites.

- *Yahooligans Search Engine* (www.yahooligans.com). Yahoo! also provides this search engine for children 7 to 12 years old.

- *Lightspan.com* (www.lightspan.com). It provides grade-by-grade recommendations about what children should know by a certain grade. Among other Lightspan.com sites are *The Global Schoolhouse* (www.gsh.org) and *Study Web* (www.studyweb.com).

While further study of student computer use is needed, some basic principles are starting to emerge from research that has been conducted among teachers and students. In particular, using the computer to prepare a presentation before an audience appeared to catch the students' interest. This seems to be the case across all levels of students—across ability levels, across socio-economic groups and across grades. Many of these projects can involve the computer for preparation of material, for example, word processing for producing the script for a play or presentation software for producing graphics.

Student engagement in learning is heightened when computers are used as one of a set of teaching tools. Integrating computer use in the learning of "substantive" subject matter (rather than "computer class") further enhances the student engagement. In studies, students were more involved where the computer was used as a tool to accomplish a task—such as word processing, Internet searching or desktop publishing.

While students' individual experiences and ability levels must be recognized since some students will have home access to computers and more advanced skills than those who do not have a home computer, use of the computer can motivate students and create a sense of accomplishment. Some studies have found that students who do not excel in a traditional setting are motivated by focused projects using the computer. Teachers have found that allowing interdisciplinary work rather than enforcing strict unit boundaries creates more student motivation. The use of virtual tours can be used in historical, cultural, social, language and geographic units.

For those of you with Internet access, we have provided Internet site listings as a place to start looking for more information about the real locations. We have provided the names of organizations, with addresses and telephone and fax numbers in some cases. Some of these organizations may have chapters that can be found in your local telephone directory.

Virtual Field Trips

The use of virtual tours of the real places in this book can help engage the children, motivating them to pursue knowledge on their own. As a precaution, we suggest that you check the Internet sites before allowing children to access them without supervision. Stay aware that the children can move to another, possibly unreviewed, site with the click of the mouse. Some sites may contain information, such as images, that might be upsetting to some children. For example, the Cyberbus site shows landmines. The pictures have been included for educational purposes but may not be appropriate for all children.

All the sites listed were visited and contained information on the subject listed at the time of writing. Computer information changes daily, however, and changes may have occurred. The inclusion of a site does not imply our endorsement of the site or its point-of-view. We have listed some general information websites here as resources in addition to those listed with the books.

For a list of all U.S. states with links to information on each, go to http://local.yahoo.com. An excellent source for a virtual field trip is www.ustrek.org/odyssey/info/index.html.

Internet Lists of Award-winning Books

- *Caldecott Winners* (www.ala.org/alsc/caldecott.html)

- *Newbery Winners* (www.ala.org/alsc/newbery.html)

- *Coretta Scott King Winners* (www.ala.org/srrt/csking)

- *Michael L. Printz Winners:* (www.ala.org/yalsa/printz)

- *Teacher's Favorites:* (www.nea.org/readacross)

- *Student's Favorites:* (www.nea.org/readacross/kidsbooks.html)

Map Sites

- *Mapquest™* (www.mapquest.com)
- *Atlapedia™ Online* (www.atlapedia.com/index.html)
- *National Geographic's Map Machine* (www.nationalgeographic.com/maps)

Sites with Country Information

- *The World Factbook 2000* (www.odci.gov/cia/publications/factbook)
- *cyberschoolbus* (www.un.org/Pubs/CyberSchoolBus/index.html)
- *National Geographic Kids* (www.nationalgeographic.com/kids/index.html)

General Information Sites

- *childslife.com* (www.childslife.com)
- *National Geographic* (www.nationalgeographic.com)
- *The History Channel* (www.historychannel.com)
- *Internet Public Library* (www.ipl.org/youth)

Language and Translation Sites

- *Translate with Babelfish* (http://babelfish.altavista.digital.com/translate.dyn)
- *Babylon.com* (www.babylon.com)
- *Dictionary.com*(www.dictionary.com/translate)
- *Free Translation* (www.freetranslation.com)
- *Learn a New Language* (www.travlang.com)

Enjoy the virtual tours and presentations the children create about and from them!

Going to Real Places

There are locations in this book that can be visited in person. Some offer tours while others are places to drive by. Because of the popularity of some of the books listed, tourist sites have developed at some locations. If planning in-person visits, call to check the details regarding hours of operation and costs or write for information. Some of the locations mentioned are non-tourist businesses. While they are open to the public, they may not welcome groups of children.

Websites for Planning In-person Visits

- *The Tourism Board* (www.towd.com) and *American Automobile Association—AAA* (www.aaa.com) are helpful for obtaining directions, maps and travel guides. Some AAA regional offices have representatives available to present automobile and bicycle safety programs to students and adults.
- *Fodor's* (www.fodors.com) and *Frommer's* (www.frommers.com) are publishers of travel guides.
- *Desteo:* (http://desteo.com) provides free travel information.

Travel/Tourism Assistance for Areas in the United States

State/Region	Tel. Number	State/Region	Tel. Number
Alabama	334-242-4169	Montana	406-444-2654
Alaska	907-465-2012	Nebraska	402-471-3794
Arizona	602-230-7733	Nevada	702-687-4322
Arkansas	501-682-1088	New Hampshire	603-271-2665
California	916-322-2881	New Jersey	609-292-6963
Colorado	303-592-5510	New Mexico	800-545-2040
Connecticut	203-258-4286	New York	800-456-8669
Delaware	800-441-8846	North Carolina	919-733-4171
Dist.of Columbia	202-789-7000	North Dakota	800-437-2077
Florida	904-488-5607	Ohio	800-282-5393
Georgia	404-656-3553	Oklahoma	405-521-3981
Hawaii	808-586-2550	Oregon	800-547-7842
Idaho	208-334-2470	Pennsylvania	800-237-4363
Illinois	312-814-4732	Rhode Island	800-845-2000
Indiana	317-232-8860	South Carolina	803-734-0122
Iowa	515-242-4705	South Dakota	800-843-1930
Kansas	913-296-2009	Tennessee	615-741-2158
Kentucky	502-564-4930	Texas	512-462-9191
Louisiana	504-568-6968	Utah	801-538-1030
Maine	207-289-5710	Vermont	208-828-3236
Maryland	410-767-6277	Virginia	804-786-2051
Massachusetts	617-727-3201	Virgin Islands	809-774-8784
Michigan	517-373-0670	Washington	360-753-5600
Minnesota	612-296-2755	West Virginia	800-225-5982
Mississippi	800-647-2290	Wisconsin	608-266-2345
Missouri	800-877-1234	Wyoming	307-777-7777

Before You Begin

Final Thoughts on the Journey

As parents or educators, we do not know in a definitive way how what we do with the children will impact their future decisions, choices, careers or lifestyles. However, by reading with a child and opening the doors to literacy, we know that we are providing a key for the child to achieve his or her potential. Sometimes, there may be road blocks or personal construction zones, but through reading stories, discussing the character's choices, learning about the diversity of locations in this country and abroad, we are offering options to our children.

There are reports in newspapers, magazines and on the radio about kids lacking problem-solving skills and seeming to flounder without confidence or career goals. Recent reports would also lead us to believe that we are in a society in which females are still not steered toward the sciences. There are books in this bibliography that can become springboards for various projects. Perhaps that one opportunity will turn a child onto science, or let that a pupil entertain the new possibilities for the future, "Yes, I can do that one day." A few examples are *Baseball Saved Us*, *Old Yeller*, *Snowflake Bentley*, *The Biggest and the Best Flag That Ever Flew*, *This Land Is Your Land*, *Through My Eyes* and *William Shakespeare and the Globe*.

Entry Format

1. Title of the book

2. Author, publisher, publication date and ISBN

3. Read aloud ages of the audience who would most enjoy listening to this story

4. About the books: book summary

5. Where you will travel: real locations in the book

6. For more information: names, addresses, phone and fax numbers, websites and email addresses for the real locations

Appendixes

Appendix A is a list of the books by read-aloud age. Appendix B is a list of the award-winning books. Appendix C contains blank U.S. and world maps.

Indexes

We provide three indexes for maximum user friendliness: author, location and title.

The Journey Begins Here

The Absolutely Essential Eloise Series

Kay Thompson. Simon & Schuster Children's, 1999. ISBN: 0689827032

Age level: 6–9

About the books: A six-year-old girl describes her busy and interesting life at the Plaza Hotel in New York City. This is one in a series about this lively little girl.

Where you will travel: Locations in the first book include The Plaza Hotel, New York City, New York; Virginia; Trafalgar Square, Piccadilly, Covent Garden and Buckingham Palace in London, England; Jamaica; Bavaria, Germany; Madrid, Spain and Paris, France.

For more information about The Plaza Hotel and New York City:

- The Plaza
  Fifth Avenue at Central Park South
  New York, NY 10019
  tel: 212-759-3000, fax: 212-546-5324
  URL: *www.fairmont.com* (choose The Plaza from the Hotels & Resorts menu)
- NYC Tourist—The Official Website for New York City Tourism
  URL: *www.nyctourist.com*

For more information about Virginia:

- Virginia Information Providers Network
  URL: *www.vipnet.org/vipnet/portal/virginia/index.htm*

For more information about London:

- The London Tourist Board
  URL: *www.londontouristboard.com*

- About.com—London
  URL: *http://london.about.com/mbody.htm*

For more information about Jamaica:

- Jamaica Tourist Board
  URL: *www.jamaicatravel.com*

For more information about Bavaria:

- Bavaria (Bayern in German)
  URL: *www.bayern.de/welcomeE.html*

For more information about Spain:

- Spain's Board of Tourism
  URL: *www.tourspain.es/inicioi.htm*

- New York Tourist Office of Spain
  666 Fifth Ave.
  New York, NY 10103
  tel: 212-265-8822

- California Tourist Office of Spain
  8383 Wilshire Blvd, Suite 960
  Beverly Hills, CA 90211
  tel: 323-658-7188, fax : 323-658-1061

For more information about Paris:

- Your French Connection
  URL: *www.yourfrenchconnexion.com/paris.html*

- Paris Pages
  URL: *www.paris.org*

Abuela

Arthur Dorros. Puffin, 1997. ISBN: 0140562257

Age level: 5–9

About the book: A granddaughter and her abuela (grandmother) love to imagine. They see many sights as they soar over Manhattan pretending to fly like the birds.

Where you will travel: They visit Central Park, the Statue of Liberty and Liberty Island and Midtown Manhattan, New York City, New York.

For more information about New York:

- New York City's Visitor Information Center
  tel: 1-800-NYC-VISIT (U.S. and Canada) or 212-397-8222 (elsewhere)

- The Dairy, Central Park Visitor Center
  Central Park near 65th St.
  tel: 212-794-6564

- NY.com (featuring neighborhoods of Manhattan)
  URL: *www.ny.com/sights/neighborhoods/ index.html*

- The Statue of Liberty National Monument
  Statue of Liberty/Ellis Foundation offices
  tel: 212-883-1986, ext. 742
  URL: *www.nps.gov/stli/mainmenu.htm*

All-of-a-Kind-Family

Sydney Taylor. Yearling Books, 1980. ISBN: 0440400597

Age level: 8–12

About the book: Spend time growing up in a big family of five girls and one boy in New York City's East Side as they go to the market or library, celebrate Jewish holidays and go about the normal business of life at the turn of the twentieth century.

Where you will travel: The main New York City locales are the Lower East Side of New York City, New York Public Library, main and branches, the East River, Rivington Street, Sheriff Street, Coney Island.

For more information about **Jewish New York:**

- The Museum of Jewish Heritage
  18 First Place
  Battery Park City
  New York, NY 10004-1484
  tel: 212-968-1800
  URL: *www.mjhnyc.org*

- Tours of the Lower East Side
  tel: 888-DRPHIL5 (888-377-4455)
  e-mail: drphil@jewishmaven.com

- Brooklyn Information and Culture—Coney Island
  URL: *http://brooklynx.org/tourism/day/neighborhood/coneyisland.asp*

- Coney Island History Site
  URL: *http://naid.sppsr.ucla.edu/coneyisland/index.html*

Amelia and Eleanor Go for a Ride

Pam Muñoz Ryan. Scholastic Trade, 1999. ISBN: 059096075X

Age level: 4–8

About the book: This picture book celebrates the courage and pioneering spirit of Amelia Earhart and Eleanor Roosevelt as they leave a dinner at the White House for a night of flying and driving.

Where you will travel: They visit the White House, the Mall and the Capitol in Washington, DC; Baltimore, Maryland; Potomac River and Chesapeake Bay. The Atlantic Ocean voyage of Amelia Earhart is discussed.

For more information about **The White House:**

- 24-hour Visitors Office Info Line
  The White House
  tel: 202-456-7041
  URL: *www.whitehouse.gov*

- The Official Tourism Website of Washington, DC
  URL: *www.washington.org*

For more information about **Amelia Earhart:**

- The Amelia Earhart Birthplace Museum
  P.O. Box 128
  Atchison, KS 66002
  e-mail: aemuseum@ispchannel.com
  URL: *http://ameliaearhartmuseum.org*

American Girl Series

Pleasant Company

Meet Addy: An American Girl (American Girls Collection Series: Addy #1)
Connie Rose Porter. Pleasant Company Publications, 1986. ISBN: 0937295019

Meet Felicity: An American Girl (American Girls Collection Series: Felicity #1)
Valerie Tripp. Pleasant Company Publications, 1991. ISBN: 1562470043

Meet Josefina: An American Girl (American Girls Collection Series: Josefina #1)
Valerie Tripp. Pleasant Company Publications, 1997. ISBN: 1562475150

Meet Kirsten (The American Girls Collection Series: Kirsten #1)
Janet Beeler Shaw. Pleasant Company Publications, 1986. ISBN: 0937295019

Meet Kit: An American Girl (American Girls Collection Series: Kit #1)
Valerie Tripp. Pleasant Company Publications, 2000. ISBN: 1584850167

Meet Molly: An American Girl (American Girls Collection Series: Molly #1)
Valerie Tripp. Pleasant Company Publications, 1986. ISBN: 0937295078

Meet Samantha: An American Girl (American Girls Collection Series: Samantha #1)
Susan S. Adler. Pleasant Company Publications, 1986. ISBN: 0937295043

Age level: 6–9

About the books: Each American Girl lives in a different historical time period and has several books about her life. Felicity lived in 1700's just before the American Revolution in Williamsburg, Virginia. Kirsten lived in 1854 and immigrated from Sweden to a rural town in Minnesota. Josefina lived on a ranch outside Santa Fe, New Mexico, in 1824. Addy lived in the 1860's during the Civil War and escaped from slavery with her mother to Philadelphia, Pennsylvania. Samantha lived in 1904 in Mount Bedford, New York. Kit lived in Cincinnati, Ohio, during the Great Depression in 1934. Molly lived in New Hampshire in 1944 during World War II.

Where you will travel: The different series take place in Williamsburg, Virginia, rural Minnesota, outside Santa Fe, New Mexico, Philadelphia, Pennsylvania, Mount Bedford, New York and Cincinnati, Ohio.

For more information about American Girls:

- The American Girls Collection
  URL: *http://www.americangirl.com/collection/collection*

For more information about Felicity's Time and Place:

- Colonial Williamsburg Foundation
  P.O. Box 1776
  Williamsburg, VA 23187-1776
  tel:1-800-404-3371
  URL: *www.history.org*

For more information about Kirsten's Time and Place:

- Gammelgården Museum
  20880 Olinda Trail
  Scandia, MN 55073
  tel: 651-433-5053
  URL: *www.scandiamn.com/gammelgarden/index.htm*

For more information about Addy's Time and Place:

- Ohio Village
  1982 Velma Ave.
  Columbus, OH 43211
  tel: 800-646-5184
  URL: *www.ohiohistory.org/places/ohvillag*

For more information about Samantha's Time and Place:

- The Historical Society of Washington, D.C.
  1307 New Hampshire Ave. NW
  Washington, DC 20036
  tel: 202-887-8936
  URL: *www.hswdc.org/samanths.htm*

For more information about Molly's Time and Place:

- The Strawbery Banke Museum
  P.O. Box 300
  Portsmouth, NH 03802
  tel: 603-433-1106
  URL: *www.strawberybanke.org*

And Then What Happened, Paul Revere?

Jean Fritz. Paper Star, 1996. ISBN: 0698113519

Age level: 8–10

About the book: This is an interesting, entertaining book about Paul Revere. It is full of facts about Paul's life before, during and after the American Revolution.

Where you will travel: Paul Revere lived and worked in Boston, Massachusetts.

For more information about Paul Revere:

- The Paul Revere House
  19 North Square
  Boston, MA 02113
  tel: 617-523-2338, fax: 617-523-1775
  URL: *www.paulreverehouse.org*

- The Old North Church
  193 Salem St.
  Boston, MA 02113-1198
  tel: 617-523-6676
  URL: *www.oldnorth.com*

For more information about Boston:

- Boston's Official Website
  URL: *www.ci.boston.ma.us*

Anne of Green Gables (series)

L.M. Montgomery. Grammercy, 1998. ISBN: 0517189682

Age level: 10–12

About the books: An older spinster and her brother send for a boy to help with the farm chores. Instead they are sent the imaginative, red-headed orphan girl, Anne Shirley. The stories tell of her adventures at Green Gables on Prince Edward Island. In real life, this farm was the home of David Jr. and Margaret MacNeill, who were cousins of the author's grandfather. Other books in the series which chronicle Anne's adventures growing up are *Anne of Avonlea, Anne of the Island, Anne of Windy Poplars, Anne's House of Dreams, Anne of Ingleside, Rainbow Valley, Chronicles of Avonlea* and *Further Chronicles of Avonlea.*

About L.M. Montgomery: Shortly after her death in 1942, Ms. Montgomery was recognized by the Historic Sites and Monuments Board of Canada as being a person of national significance and a monument and plaque were erected at Green Gables.

Where you will travel: Green Gables, located in Cavendish, Prince Edward Island, Canada, is a popular tourist destination.

For more information about Green Gables:

- Ardgowan National Historic Site
  2 Palmers Ln.
  Charlottetown, Prince Edward Island
  Canada C1A 5V6
  tel: 902-566-7050, fax: 902-566-7226
  e-mail: atlantic_parksinfo@pch.gc.ca

- The Anne of Green Gables Society
  Kindred Spirits
  Dept. C, Box 491
  Avonlea, Prince Edward Island
  Canada C0B 1M0
  tel: 1-800-665-2663
  Email: kindredspirits@annesociety.org
  URL: *www.annesociety.org*

Arthur Meets the President

Marc Brown. Little Brown & Co., 1992. ISBN: 0316112917

Age level: 4–8

About the book: Arthur wins an essay contest and is chosen to visit the White House. In her own way, his sister D.W. saves the day.

Where you will travel: The White House is located at 1600 Pennsylvania Avenue, Washington, D.C.

For more information about The White House:

- Online Tour of the White House
  URL: *www.whitehouse.gov/history/whtour/index.html*

- For information on real-life tours, call
  The 24-hour Visitors Office Info Line
  tel: 202-456-7041

- How to Tour the White House
  URL: *www.whitehouse.gov/tours/index.html*

Aunt Flossie's Hats (and Crab Cakes Later)

Elizabeth Fitzgerald Howard. Clarion Books, 1995. ISBN: 039572077X

Age level: 5–9

About the book: Two girls love to visit Aunt Flossie. As the girls try on Aunt Flossie's hats, she tells them a story about each one.

Where you will travel: Aunt Flossie lives in Baltimore, Maryland.

For more information about Baltimore:

- Baltimore, Maryland Welcomes You
  URL: *www.ci.baltimore.md.us*

- The Baltimore Area Convention and Visitors Association (BACVA)
  100 Light St.
  Baltimore, MD 21202
  tel: 888-Baltimore or 800-343-3468

The Ballot Box Battle

Emily Arnold McCully . Alfred A. Knopf, 1996. ISBN-0-679-87938-2

Age level: 5-9

About the book: It is Election Day of 1880 and Elizabeth Cady Stanton decides to try and cast her ballot. At first, her young companion is embarrassed by Elizabeth's actions, but later the girl is empowered by Stanton's courage.

Where you will travel: Elizabeth Cady Stanton lived on Highwood Avenue in Tenafly, New Jersey, from 1868 to 1880.

For more information about Tenafly, New Jersey:

- Important Facts about Tenafly
  URL: *www.tenaflynj.org/facts.html*

- The Tenafly Historic Preservation Commission
  tel: 201-568-6100

For more information about Women's Rights:

- The Women's Rights National Historic Park
  Seneca Falls, NY
  tel: 315-568-2991
  URL: *www.nps.gov/wori/home.htm*

- The Elizabeth Cady Stanton House in the Park, is open for tours.

- The Elizabeth Cady Stanton & Susan B. Anthony Papers Project Online
  URL: *http://ecssba.rutgers.edu*

- Department of History,
  Rutgers, The State University of New Jersey
  16 Seminary Place
  New Brunswick, NJ 08901-1108

Baseball Saved Us

Ken Mochizuki. Lee & Low Books, 1995. ISBN: 1880000199

Age level: 9–12

About the book: After the attack on Pearl Harbor, a Japanese boy (nicknamed "Shorty") and his family are forced to live in an internment camp. Father and son use baseball as a way to escape the realities of the camp, even if only for nine innings. What will happen when Shorty goes to bat in the final inning of the championship game?

About Japanese internment camps: The anniversary of Japanese Internment is February 19. In 1942, Executive Order 9066 resulted in approximately 110,000 Japanese-Americans who lived on the West Coast being placed in internment camps in isolated areas of Arizona, Arkansas, inland California, Colorado, Idaho, Utah and Wyoming. The first phase moved them into assembly centers, which were makeshift detention camps at fairgrounds, racetracks and labor camps. On January 2, 1945, they were allowed to return to their homes. Two-thirds of the interned were U.S. citizens.

Where you will travel: The book takes place in or discusses Japan; Pearl Harbor, Hawaii; Minidoka Camp (internment camp) in Idaho.

For more information about Japanese Internment Camps:

- The National Japanese American Historical Society
  1684 Post St.
  San Francisco, CA 94115
  tel: 415-921-5007, fax: 415-921-5087
  e-mail: njahs@njahs.org

For more information about Japan at War:

- Japan at War, 1932–1945
  URL: *www.danford.net/japan.htm*

- Electric Library's Encyclopedia.com—Pearl Harbor article
  URL: *www.encyclopedia.com/articles/09951.html*

For more information about the USS Missouri:

- Visitor Information to the USS Missouri (BB-63)
  tel: 877-MIGHTY-MO or 888-USS-MISSOURI

Beautiful Warrior: The Legend of the Nun's Kung Fu

Emily Arnold McCully. Scholastic Trade, 1998. ISBN: 0590374877

Age level: 6–9

About the book: A nun becomes a martial arts master. She helps a young girl fend off an unruly suitor and find a new way of life.

Where you will travel: The nun lives in the Shaolin Monastery during the Ming dynasty of China in 1644, near The Great Wall of China.

For more information about the Ming Dynasty and Ming, China:

- Timeline 17th Century
  URL: *www.magicdragon.com/UltimateSF/timeline17.html*

- Washington State University—World Civilizations
  URL: *www.wsu.edu:8080/~dee/MING/MING1.HTM*

For more information about The Great Wall:

- The University of Maine at Farmington's Great Wall Page
  URL: *http://zinnia.umfacad.maine.edu/~mshea/China/great.html*

For more information about the Shaolin Monastery:

- Peter M. Geiser's Internet Travel Guide
  URL: *www.pmgeiser.ch/china/places/shaolin.htm*

Ben and Me: An Astonishing Life of Benjamin Franklin as Written by His Good Mouse Amos

Robert Lawson. Little Brown & Co., 1988. ISBN: 0316517305

Age level: 8–10

About the book: The reader observes Benjamin Franklin's accomplishments through the eyes of his Good Mouse Amos. Amos lives with Benjamin Franklin and takes credit for Franklin's inventions.

Where you will travel: Benjamin Franklin's home was in Philadelphia, Pennsylvania. Ben Franklin's home and workplace are located in Independence National Historic Park on Market Street between 3rd and 4th Streets.

For more information about Benjamin Franklin and his home:

- Independence National Historical Park
  313 Walnut St.
  Philadelphia, PA 19106
  URL: *www.nps.gov/inde/exindex.htm*

The Biggest and Best Flag That Ever Flew

Rebecca C. Jones. Cornell Maritime Press, Inc., 1994. ISBN: 0870334409

Age level: 6–9

About the book: Caroline Pickersgill, her mother and her grandmother sew the American Flag that flew over Fort McHenry and inspired Francis Scott Key to write The Star Spangled Banner.

Where you will travel: You'll visit Albemarle St. in Baltimore, Maryland; Fort McHenry, Maryland; Washington, D.C. and Great Britain.

For more information about the American Flag:

- The Star Spangled Banner Flag House
  844 East Pratt St.
  Baltimore, MD 21202
  tel: 410-837-1793, fax: 410-837-1812
  e-mail: info@flaghouse.org
  URL: *www.flaghouse.org*

- National Museum of American History
  Smithsonian Institution Visitor Information
  Washington, D.C. 20560
  tel: 202-357-2700 (voice) or 202-357-1729 (TTY)
  URL: *http://americanhistory.si.edu*

Bingleman's Midway

Karen Ackerman. Boyds Mills Press, 1995. ISBN: 156397366

Age level: 6–9

About the book: A boy is a non-believer in magic at the carnival until he sees Bingleman's show. As he tries to run away and join the carnival that night, his father is there and is sympathetic to his desires. Discover the wonders of a summer carnival.

Where you will travel: The carnival is set up on Route 66 in Ohio.

For more information about Route 66:

- The National Historic Route 66 Federation
  P.O. Box 423, Dept. WS
  Tujunga, CA 91043-0423
  tel and fax: 818-352-7232
  e-mail: national66@national66.com

- Ohio State Route 66 Internet Tour (virtual tour)
  URL: *www.geocities.com/Heartland/Acres/2153/66.html.*

Bloomers!

Rhoda Blumberg. Aladdin Paperbacks, 1996. ISBN: 0689804555

Age level: 5–9

About the book: Beginning in the 1850's, one woman's visit to Seneca Falls started a fashion trend. That trend helped to spread the word about women's rights.

Where you will travel: The book takes place in Seneca Falls, New York and the mountains of Switzerland.

For more information about the history of Women's Rights:

- The National Women's Hall of Fame
  76 Fall St., P.O. Box 335
  Seneca Falls, NY 13148
  tel: 315-568-8060, fax: 315-568-2976
  e-mail: greatwomen@greatwomen.org
  URL: *www.greatwomen.org/bloomr.htm*

For more information about Seneca Falls:

- The Heritage Area's Visitor Center
  115 Fall St.
  Seneca Falls, NY 13148

- Seneca Falls Online
  URL: *www.senecafallsonline.com*

For more information about skiing in Switzerland:

- Skiswitzerland.com
  URL: *www.skiswitzerland.com*

Blueberries for Sal

Robert McCloskey. Viking Press, 1976. ISBN: 014050169X

Age level: 3–6

About the book: A little girl and her mother go to pick blueberries one bright summer day. To her surprise, the little girl discovers she is not the only one picking blueberries with her mother.

Where you will travel: The story takes place in Maine, where Cherryfield is the blueberry capital of the world.

For more information about Maine blueberry picking:

- Maine Office of Tourism
  tel: 800-533-9595

The Boston Coffee Party

Doreen Rappaport. HarperCollins Children's Books, 1990. ISBN: 0064441415

Age level: 7–11

About the book: Based on a true story, women and children take charge of things as a greedy merchant tries to inflate coffee prices. Told from a child's perspective, this Revolutionary War story includes the reality of sugar sold in bulk, of jam made from scratch, of clothes cut and stitched by hand, of war shortages and of absent fathers.

Where you will travel: The story takes place in Boston, Massachusetts, particularly Corn Hill.

For more information about the Boston Tea Party:

- Boston Tea Party Ships and Museum
  Congress Street Bridge
  Boston, MA 02210
  tel: 617-338-1773
  URL: *www.bostonteapartyship.com*

- The Boston National Historical Park
  Charlestown Navy Yard
  Boston, MA 02129
  tel: 617-242-5642
  e-mail: bost_email@nps
  URL: *www.nps.gov/bost/home.htm*

For more information about Boston:

- Boston's Official Website
  URL: *www.ci.boston.ma.us*

Bound for Oregon

Jean Van Leeuwen. Puffin, 1996. ISBN: 0140383190

Age level: 10–12

About the book: A nine-year old girl tells of her trip on the Oregon Trail in the 1850's, including realistic descriptions of both the good and bad events on the Trail in that era. This story is based on the account of Mary Jane Todd's journey from Arkansas to Oregon.

Where you will travel: Their journey began in Arkansas and continued from Independence, Missouri, through Nebraska, Wyoming and Idaho to Oregon.

For more information about the Oregon Trail:

- Overland-Oregon Trail Outposts
  URL: *www.over-land.com*
  Links you to sites about the locations along both the Overland and the Oregon Trails. The Trail West links to many sites related to the Oregon Trail.

- The University of Kansas' Oregon Trail Page
  URL: *www.ukans.edu/kansas/seneca/oregon*

- National Historic Oregon Trail Interpretive Center at Flagstaff Hill
  Oregon Highway 86
  P.O. Box 987
  Baker City, OR 97814-0987
  tel: 541-523-1843, fax: 541-523-1834
  URL: *www.or.blm.gov/NHOTIC*

- The Trails Project (virtual visit)
  URL: *http://trails.kcmsd.k12.mo.us/homepage.htm*

The Bracelet

Yoshiko Uchida. The Putnam Publishing Group, 1996. ISBN: 069811390X

Age level: 7–11

About the book: Before leaving for an internment camp, a Japanese-American girl is given a gift so that she will remember her best friend forever.

About Japanese internment camps: The anniversary of Japanese Internment is February 19. In 1942, Executive Order 9066 resulted in approximately 110,000 Japanese-Americans who lived on the West Coast being placed in internment camps in isolated areas of Arizona, Arkansas, inland California, Colorado, Idaho, Utah and Wyoming. The first phase moved them into assembly centers that were makeshift detention camps at fairgrounds, racetracks and labor camps On January 2, 1945, they were allowed to return to their homes. Two-thirds of the interned were U.S. citizens.

Where you will travel: Berkeley, Tanforan Racetracks and San Francisco Bay Bridge, all in California, are the locations in the story. Tanforan Racetracks, currently the site of Tanforan Park Shopping Center, was one of the "assembly centers."

For more information about Japanese Internment Camps:

- The National Japanese American Historical Society
  1684 Post St.
  San Francisco, CA 94115
  tel: 415-921-5007, fax: 415-921-5087
  e-mail: njahs@njahs.org.

Caddie Woodlawn

Carol Ryrie Brink. Aladdin Paperbacks, 1997. ISBN: 0689815212

Age level: 8–10

About the book: In 1857, F. John Woodhouse, with his wife Harriet and their five children, moved from Boston, to 160 rugged acres in the Wisconsin wilderness. Caddie, a tomboy, loves her new home. The story is based on the author's grandmother, Caroline Augusta Woodhouse.

Where you will travel: The story is about the family's new life in Dunn County, Wisconsin.

For more information about Caddie Woodlawn and Dunn County, Wisconsin:

- The Dunn County Historical Society
  P.O. Box 437
  Menomonie, WI 54751
  tel: 715-232-8685
  URL: *www.discover-net.com/~dchs/sitecw.html*

- The Caddie Woodlawn Historical Park and Wayside
  Located nine miles south of Menomonie on Highway 25.

Casey Jones' Fireman: The story of Sim Webb

Nancy Farmer. Phyllis Fogelman Books, 1999. ISBN: 0803719299

Age level: 6–9

About the book: Sim Webb is the fireman for the legendary Casey Jones. The railroad fireman senses danger, but follows the legendary engineer's command to make the Cannon Ball Express go faster.

Where you will travel: Memphis, Tennessee, is the location.

For more information about Memphis, Tennessee:

- The City of Memphis Website
  URL: *www.ci.memphis.tn.us/visitor_info/main.cfm*

For more information about Casey Jones:

- The Casey Jones Village
  56 Casey Jones Ln.
  Jackson TN, 38305
  tel: 800-748-9588, fax: 901-668-6889
  URL: *http://casey@caseyjonesvillage.com*

- The Casey Jones Railroad Museum State Park
  10091 Vaughan Rd. #1
  Vaughan, MS 39179
  tel: 662-673-9864

Chicken Soup With Rice

Maurice Sendak. HarperTrophy, 1991. ISBN: 006443253X

Age level: 4–8

About the book: This book contains 12 poems about a boy's journey through the months of the year and the ways he enjoys eating chicken soup with rice. This is an appropriate book to read during September, which is Soup and Sandwich Month or January because that is National Soup Month.

Where you will travel: The book journeys in Spain and Mumbai (Bombay), India and along the Nile River, Egypt.

For more information about Spain:

- Spain's Board of Tourism
  URL: *www.tourspain.es/inicioi.htm*

- The New York Tourist Office of Spain
  666 Fifth Ave.
  New York, NY 10103
  tel: 212-265-8822

- Contact the California Tourist Office of Spain
  8383 Wilshire Blvd, Suite 960
  Beverly Hills, CA 90211
  tel: 323-658-7188, fax: 323-658-1061

For more information about Mumbai, India:

- Mumbai on the Net
  e-mail: info@mumbainet.com
  URL: *www.mumbainet.com*

For more information about the Nile River:

- NileRiver.com
  URL: *www.nileriver.com*

- The Living Africa—Nile River
  URL: *http://library.thinkquest.org/16645/the_land/nile_river.shtml*

Dave at Night

Gail Carson Levine. HarperTrophy, 2001. ISBN: 0064407470

Age level: 11 and up

About the book: A boy is put in an orphanage and sneaks out at night. An older gentleman befriends him and together they explore the New York City of the Harlem Renaissance of 1920-30.

Where you will travel: The book moves through New York City (including the Borough of Queens; the Queensboro Bridge; on the Lower East Side, Canal St. and Grand St.; Broadway and Amsterdam Ave., Convent Ave., Stanton Street, Delancey St., the Waldorf Hotel; St. Nicholas Park and Harlem); Chicago, Illinois; Jersey City and Trenton, New Jersey; California; Greece; Turkey and Yiddish areas of Russia and Germany.

For more information about New York:

- New York Convention & Visitors Bureau
  Visitor Information Center
  810 Seventh Ave.
  New York, NY 10019
  tel: 1-800-NYC-VISIT (U.S. and Canada) or 212-397-8222 (elsewhere)
  URL: *www.nycvisit.com*

- Multilingual Visitor Information Counselor
  tel: 212-484-1222

- Queens Tourism Director
  tel: 718-286-2663
  e-mail: info@queensbp.org

- Neighborhood Heritage Tour
  Lower East Side Tenement Museum
  URL: *www.tenement.org/tours.html*

- The Waldorf Astoria Hotel
  301 Park Ave.
  New York, NY 10022-6897
  tel: 800-WALDORF
  URL: *www.hilton.com/en/hi/hotels/information.jhtml?ctyhocn=NYCWAHH&key=HOME*

- Encarta Schoolhouse—Harlem Renaissance
  URL: *http://encarta.msn.com/schoolhouse/harlem/harlem.asp*

- New Jersey State Museum
  205 West State St.
  P.O. Box 530
  Trenton, NJ 08625-0530
  tel: 609-292-6464

For more information about Chicago, Illinois:

- The City of Chicago
  tel: 800-226-6632
  URL: *www.ci.chi.il.us*

For more information about Yiddish:

- The Yiddish Voice
  WUNR,
  160 N. Washington St.
  Boston, MA 02114
  tel: 617-738-1870, fax: 617-249-0141
  e-mail: yv@world.std.com
  URL: *www.yiddishvoice.com*

For more information about touring Greece and Turkey:

- Avenir Travel & Adventures
  2029 Sidewinder Drive

P.O. Box 2730
Park City, UT 84060
tel: 800-367-3230, fax: 435-649-1192
URL: *www.meanderadventures.com*

The Fiddler of the Northern Lights

Natalie Kinsey-Warnock. Dutton Children's Books, 1996. ISBN: 0525652159

Age level: 5–9

About the book: A family lives in the Northern woods. No one believes the stories grandpa tells about the Northern woods except his grandson until one adventurous night. This story has an underlying theme of family members sharing stories with each other and the bonds that sharing forms.

Where you will travel: Their adventure is along the St. Maurice River in eastern Quebec, Canada.

For more information about the Northern Lights:

- The Aurora Page
  URL: *www.geo.mtu.edu/weather/aurora*

- The Aurora
  URL: *www.pfrr.alaska.edu/~pfrr/AURORA/INDEX.HTM*

- Northern Lights (from Norway)
  URL: *www.northern-lights.no*

For more information about Quebec, Canada:

- Bonjour Quebec
  tel: 877-266-5687
  URL: *www.tourisme.gouv.qc.ca*

The Fortune Tellers

Lloyd Alexander. Penguin USA, 1992. ISBN: 0525448497

Age level: 6–9

About the book: A man goes to a fortuneteller to find out what he will do in the future instead of being a carpenter. The predictions come true in an unusual way.

Where you will travel: The story takes place in Cameroon in Africa.

For more information about Cameroon:

- The Republic of Cameroon—Michael T. Fosong
  URL: *www.compufix.demon.co.uk/camweb*

- West-Africa.com
  URL: *www.west-africa.com/cameroon/cameroon.htm*

From the Mixed Up Files of Mrs. Basil E. Frankweiler

E.L. Konigsburg. Aladdin Paperbacks, 1987. ISBN: 0689711816

Age level: 9–12

About the book: A sister and brother run away to live in the Metropolitan Museum of Art in New York City. They try to solve a mystery that introduces them to Mrs. Basil E. Frankweiler.

Where you will travel: The locations in the book are Greenwich, New Haven, Hartford, Farmington, Darien and Stamford, Connecticut; Grand Central Station, Grand Central Post Office, United Nations, Central Park, Metropolitan Museum; 125th Street, Madison Avenue, 80th Street, East 63rd Street, Fifth Avenue, the Theater District, Broadway, Bloomingdale's and Macy's Department Stores, the New York Public Library and the Donnell Branch Library on 53rd Street in New York City; Port Chester, New York; Marblehead, Massachusetts; Mankato, Kansas; Paris, France; the Sistine Chapel, Rome and Bologna, Italy; Egypt and Japan.

For more information about Connecticut:

- The Darien Community Information Network
  c/o Darien Library, 35 Leroy Ave.
  Darien, CT 06820-4497
  tel: 203-655-1234

- Contact the New Haven Mayor's Office
  165 Church St.
  New Haven, CT 06510
  tel: 203-946-7671, fax: 203-946-5750
  URL: *www.cityofnewhaven.com*

- Commonwealth Communities
  Town of Marblehead, Essex County
  URL: *www.state.ma.us/cc/marblehead.html*

- Marblehead.com
  URL: *www.marblehead.com*

For more information about the Metropolitan Museum of Art:

- The Metropolitan Museum of Art
  1000 Fifth Ave. at 82nd St.
  New York, NY 10028-0198
  URL: *www.metmuseum.org/home.asp*

For more information about Grand Central Station in New York:

- Grand Central Station
  Park Ave. at 42nd St.
  New York, NY 10017
  tel: 212-535-7710

- New York City Transit
  URL: *www.mta.nyc.ny.us/mnr/html/gct.htm*

For more information about Central Park in New York:

- The Central Park Conservancy
  14 E. 60th St.
  New York, NY 10022
  tel: 212-310-6600
  URL: *www.centralparknyc.org*

For more information about the United Nations:

- The United Nations
  1st Ave. at 46th St.
  New York, NY 10017
  tel: 212-963-7713
  URL: *www.un.org*

For more information about the New York Public Library:

- New York Public Library
  5th Ave. and 42nd St.
  New York, NY 10018
  tel: 212-221-7676
  URL: *www.nypl.org*

For more information about Kansas:

- Access Kansas
  URL: *www.accesskansas.org*

For more information about Paris:

- Your French Connexion
  URL: *www.yourfrenchconnexion.com/paris.html*

- The Paris Pages
  URL: *www.paris.org*

For more information about the Cistine Chapel:

- Michelangelo's Ceiling
  URL: *www.christusrex.org/www1/sistine/0-Ceiling.html*

For more information about Bologna:

- Information about Bologna (Italy)
  The Italian Tourist Web Guide
  URL: *www.itwg.com/ct_00007.asp*

For more information about Egypt:

- Egypt's State Information Service
  URL: *www.sis.gov.eg*

For more information about Japan:

- The Japan National Tourist Organization
  URL: *www.jnto.go.jp*

Hannah and the Whistling Teakettle

Mindy Warshaw Skolsky. DK Publishing, 2000. ISBN: 0789426021

Age level: 5–9

About the book: Hannah brings a new teakettle as the perfect gift for the grandmother that never wants anything. Her grandmother deems this gift unnecessary until the teakettle saves the day.

Where you will travel: The George Washington Bridge; Liberty Street School in Nyack; the Bronx the A subway in New York City and the Henry Hudson River are all in New York State.

For more information about the George Washington Bridge:

- Crossing the Hudson River
  URL: *www.inventionfactory.com/history/RHAbridg/gwbuild*

For more information about the Hudson River:

- The Hudson Valley Children's Museum
  21 Burd St.
  Nyack, NY 10960
  tel: 914-358-2191, fax: 914-358-2642
  e-mail: hvcm95@worldnet.att.net

- Contact Hudson River Trails,
  NY/NJ Trail Conference
  tel: 212-685-9699
  URL: *www.nynjtc.org*

For more information about New York subways:

- New York Transit Museum
  tel: 718-243-8601

- The Metropolitan Transportation Authority
  URL: *www.mta.nyc.ny.us*

Horton Hatches the Egg

Dr. Seuss. Random House, 1968. ISBN: 039480077X

Age level: 4–8

About the book: This is a story about a dedicated elephant who makes a commitment and sticks to it even when he is teased and when the weather is cold and rainy. He gets rewarded in the end.

Where you will travel: Characters visit or pass through Palm Beach, Florida; New York Harbor, New York; Boston, Massachusetts; Kalamazoo, Michigan; Chicago, Illinois; Weehawken, New Jersey; Washington, D.C.; Dayton, Ohio; St. Paul, Minnesota; Drake, North Dakota and Wichita, Kansas.

For more information about Palm Beach, Florida:

- Palm Beach County Convention and Visitor's Bureau
  1555 Palm Beach Lakes Blvd., Suite 204
  West Palm Beach, FL 33401
  tel: 561-233-3000, fax: 561-471-3990
  URL: *www.palmbeachfl.com*

For more information about New York, New York:

- New York Convention & Visitors Bureau
  Visitor Information Center
  810 Seventh Ave.
  New York, NY 10019
  tel: 1-800-NYC-VISIT (U.S. and Canada) or 212-397-8222 (elsewhere)
  URL: *www.nycvisit.com*

For more information about Boston, Massachusetts:

- City of Boston
  URL: *www.ci.boston.ma.us*

For more information about Kalamazoo, Michigan:

- Kalamazoo County Government
  URL: *www.kalcounty.com*

For more information about Chicago, Illinois:

- The City of Chicago
  tel: 800-226-6632
  URL: *www.ci.chi.il.us*

For more information about Weehawken, New Jersey:

- Friends of the Weehawken Waterfront
  P.O. Box 5167
  Weehawken, NJ 07087
  tel: 201-223-1378

For more information about Washington, D.C.:

- Official Tourism Website of Washington D.C.
  URL: *www.washington.org*

For more information about Dayton, Ohio:

- Official City of Dayton Website
  URL: *www.ci.dayton.oh.us*

For more information about St. Paul, Minnesota:

- Official City of St. Paul Website
  URL: *www.stpaul.gov*

For more information about Drake, North Dakota:

- The Drake, North Dakota Resource Guide
  URL: *www.pe.net/~rksnow/ndcountydrake.htm*

For more information about Wichita, Kansas:

- Official City of Wichita Website
  URL: *www.wichitagov.org*

How to Make Apple Pie and See the World

Marjorie Priceman. Random House, 1994. ISBN: 0679880836

Age level: 6–9

About the book: Follow a child on a trip around the world as she gathers the ingredients necessary to bake an apple pie. As a bonus, the recipe is included at the end of the book.

Where you will travel: The ingredients come from Italy (wheat), France (eggs), Sri Lanka (cinnamon), Jamaica (sugar) and Vermont (apples) with travel over the Indian Ocean and the English countryside.

For more information about Italian pasta:

- La Pasta
  URL: *www.pasta.it*

For more information about France's egg industry:

- The International Egg Commission
  URL: *www.internationalegg.com*

For more information about cinnamon:

- Cinnamon in Sri Lanka
  171 Galle Rd.
  Ratmalana, Mount Lavinia, Sri Lanka
  e-mail: gpds@pan.lk

For more information about sugar technology:

- Sugar Technology On-line News
  URL: *www.sucrose.com/news.html*

- Sugaronline.com
  URL: *http://sugaronline.com*

For more information about Vermont apples:

- The Apple Barn
  tel: 888- 8APPLES, fax: 802-447-0509
  e-mail: info@theapplebarn.com
  URL: *http://theapplebarn.com*

Huckabuck Family and How They Raised Popcorn in Nebraska and Quit and Came Back

Carl Sandburg. Farrar, Straus & Giroux, 1999. ISBN: 0374335117

Age level: 4–8

About the book: In this picture-book version of the classic Rootabaga story, a family must move when a fire starts and their enormous popcorn harvest pops them out of house and farm. After traveling to other towns, the family finally decides to return home. This will be a happy introduction to Sandburg for many children.

Where you will travel: The Huckabuck family travels through Nebraska; Oskaloosa, Iowa; Paducah, Kentucky; Defiance, Ohio; Indianapolis, Indiana; Walla Walla, Washington and Elgin and Peoria, Illinois.

For more information about Nebraska corn:

- The Nebraska Corn Growers Association
  1327 H St., Suite 305
  Lincoln, NE 68508
  tel: 888-CORNGRW, fax: 402-438-7241

- The North Central Development Center, Inc.
  Ainsworth Area Chamber of Commerce
  335 North Main
  P.O. Box 112
  Ainsworth, NE 69210
  tel: 402-387-2740
  e-mail: ncdc@bloomnet.com

For more information about Oskaloosa, Iowa:

- The Oskaloosa Visitor's Information Center
  124 North Market St.
  Oskaloosa, IA 52577
  URL: *www.oskaloosaiowa.org*

For more information about Padukah, Kentucky:

- The Padukah, Kentucky Recreation Website
  URL: *www.starcities.com/usa/ky/paducah/recreation.shtml*

For more information about Walla Walla, Washington:

- Walla Walla On-line
  URL: *www.ohwy.com/wa/w/wallawal.htm*

For more information about Indianapolis, Indiana:

- The City of Indianapolis and Marion County
  City-County Building
  200 East Washington St.
  Indianapolis, IN 46204
  tel: 317-327-4MAC
  URL: *www.ci.indianapolis.in.us*

For more information about Illinois' counties:

- United States Counties—Illinois Page
  URL: *www.saintclair.org/counties/state_il.html*

For more information about Defiance, Ohio:

- Defiance, Ohio Website
  URL: *www.defianceweb.com*

In the Year of the Boar and Jackie Robinson

Bette Bao Lord. Harper Collins, 1984. ISBN: 0064401758

Age level: 8–12

About the book: Set in Brooklyn, New York in 1947, an immigrant girl adapts to life in the city. Baseball becomes her passion and helps her assimilate in her new country.

Where you will travel: The book's locations include Shanghai, Chongquing (Chungking) and the Great Wall in China; San Francisco, California; Chattanooga, Tennessee; Ebbets Field and the Brooklyn Bridge, in the Borough of Brooklyn in New York City, New York and North Carolina.

For more information about Chinese Pronunciation:

- The International Museum of the Horse—Pronunciation Guide
  URL: *www.imh.org/imh/china/ed/pronounce.html*

For more information about the Great Wall:

- TravelChinaGuide.com
  URL: *www.travelchinaguide.com/cityguides/beijing/greatwall.htm*

- Great Wall Photos
  URL: *http://pasture.ecn.purdue.edu/~agenhtml/agenmc/china/scenery.html*

For more information about Chongquing and Shanghai:

- City of Seattle's Intergovernmental Relations Website
  URL: *www.cityofseattle.net/seattle/oir/chongqin.htm*

- Shanghai On-line
  URL: *www.sh.com*

For more information about San Francisco:

- The San Francisco Convention and Visitors Bureau
  URL: *www.sfvisitor.org*

For more information about Chattanooga, Tennessee:

- Chattanooga On-line
  URL: *www.chattanooga.net*

For more information about Brooklyn in New York City:

- Ballparks.com—Ebbets Field
  URL: *www.ballparks.com/baseball/national/ebbets.htm*

- Brooklyn On-line
  URL: *www.brooklynon-line.com*

- The Brooklyn Bridge Website
  URL: *www.endex.com/gf/buildings/bbridge/bbridge.html*

For more information about North Carolina:

- The Official State of North Carolina Website
  e-mail: ncgov@ncmail.net
  URL: *www.ncgov.com*

- Institute of Government
  CB# 3330 Knapp Building
  The University of North Carolina at Chapel Hill
  Chapel Hill, NC 27599-3330
  tel: 919-966-5381

Jambo Means Hello: Swahili Alphabet Book

Muriel Feelings. Penguin USA, 1974. ISBN: 0140546529

Age level: 5–9

About the book: For each of the 24 letters in the Swahili alphabet, a word in Swahili is provided. For each letter, the reader learns an aspect of this vibrant African culture.

Where you will travel: Kenya, Uganda, The People's Republic of the Congo (Zaire), Somalia, Tanzania, Rwanda, Burundi, Zambia, Malawi, Mozambique and the Malagasy Republic.

For more information about Swahili, Tanzania and eastern Africa:

- Swahili.com
  URL: *www.Swahili.com*

- Mytravelguide.com—Tanzania
  URL: *www.mytravelguide.com/countries/tanzania*

- Columbia University's LibraryWeb—African Studies "East Africa"
  URL: *www.cc.columbia.edu/cu/libraries/indiv/area/Africa/East.html*

For more information about central Africa:

- Africa South of the Sahara's Democratic Republic of Congo
  URL: *www-sul.stanford.edu/depts/ssrg/africa/zaire.html*

Johnny Tremain

Esther Forbes. Dell, 1968. ISBN: 0440442508

Age level: 10–12

About the book: Johnny Tremain is a young man who participates in the events leading up to the American Revolution. He joins the Sons of Liberty and takes part in the Boston Tea Party.

Where you will travel: The story takes place in and around Boston, Concord and Lexington, Massachusetts.

For more information about the Boston Tea Party:

- Boston Tea Party Ships and Museum
  Congress Street Bridge
  Boston, MA 02210
  tel: 617-338-1773
  URL: *www.bostonteapartyship.com*

- The Boston National Historical Park
  Charlestown Navy Yard
  Boston, MA 02129
  tel: 617-242-5642 or 617-242-5601
  e-mail: bost_email@nps
  URL: *www.nps.gov/bost/home.htm*

For more information about Boston:

* Boston's Official Website
  URL: *www.ci.boston.ma.us*

Journey to Freedom

Courtni C. Wright. Holiday House, 1994. ISBN: 0823413330

Age level: 5–9

About the book: Follow a family for twenty tense and fearful days as they travel from Kentucky to Canada with Harriet Tubman as their "conductor" on the Underground Railroad.

Where you will travel: Lexington, Kentucky; Sandusky, Ohio; Lake Erie and Ontario, Canada are the specific places in this story.

For more information about Kentucky and the Underground Railroad:

* Kentucky Educational Television—Underground Railroad
  URL: *www.ket.org/underground*

For more information about Sandusky, Ohio:

* The Sandusky Visitors Bureau
  4424 Milan Rd., Suite A
  Sandusky, OH 44870
  URL: *www.sandusky.net*

* Erie County Visitor's Bureau
  tel: 800-255-ERIE, fax: 419-625-5009
  e-mail: vcbstaff@buckeyenorth.com

For more information about Lake Erie:

* Lake Erie Binational Public Forum
  URL: *www.erieforum.org/lakeerie.html*

For information about the Underground Railroad:

* The Underground Railroad in Canada
  URL: *http://collections.ic.gc.ca/heirloom_series/volume4/264-267.htm*

  National Geographic—The Underground Railroad Resources and Links
  URL: *www.nationalgeographic.com/features/99/railroad/randl.html*

The Legend of Sleepy Hollow

Washington Irving. Penguin Putnam Books for Young Readers, 1999. ISBN: 0698116488

Age level: 10–12

About the book: A headless horseman scares off a timid suitor in this story that is set in the Hudson River Valley in the early 1800s.

Where you will travel: Sleepy Hollow was a fictional town in the lower Hudson River Valley, New York. In 1996, a quiet Hudson River village, 25 miles north of Manhattan officially renamed itself "Sleepy Hollow."

For more information about the Hudson River Valley and Sleepy Hollow:

* Historic Hudson Valley
  URL: *www.hudsonvalley.org*

- The Village of Sleepy Hollow
  28 Beekman Ave.
  Sleepy Hollow, NY 10591
  tel: 914-631-1440

- The Sleepy Hollow Society
  URL: *http://members.aol.com/sleepy129/sh/shs.htm*

Little House on the Prairie

Laura Ingalls Wilder. Harper Collins, 1971. ISBN: 0064400026

Age level: 8–12

About the books: The Little House on the Prairie series chronicles the life of a Pioneer girl, Laura, and her family. Laura grew up in the woods of Wisconsin and moved to the western frontier in the 1800's. This wonderful account of pioneer life is based on the actual events of Laura Ingalls Wilder's family. Other books in the Little House series are *Little House in the Big Woods, On the Banks of Plum Creek, Farmer Boy, The Long Winter, By the Shores of Silver Lake, Little Town on the Prairie* and *These Happy Golden Years.*

Where you will travel: "Pa" Charles Phillip Ingalls was born in Cuba, New York. "Ma" Caroline Lake Quiner was born in Brookfield, Wisconsin. Charles Ingalls and Caroline Quiner were married in Concord, Wisconsin. Mary Amelia and Laura Elizabeth Ingalls were born in Pepin, Wisconsin. Caroline Celestia Ingalls (Carrie) was born in Independence, Kansas. Charles Frederick Ingalls (Freddie) is born Walnut Grove, Minnesota. Grace Pearl Ingalls was born in Burr Oak, Iowa. Laura Ingalls and Almanzo James Wilder were married in De Smet, South Dakota, where Rose Wilder was born and Charles and Caroline Ingalls died. Mary attended the Iowa College for the Blind in Vinton, Iowa. Laura, Almanzo and Rose lived in Spring Valley, Minnesota and Westville, Florida, before settling in Mansfield, Missouri, where the books were written.

For more information about the locations in the Little House books:

- The Definitive Laura Ingalls Web Pages
  URL: *www.pinc.com/~jenslegg*

- The Laura Ingalls Wilder Memorial Society, Inc.
  P.O Box 426
  De Smet, SD 57231
  tel: 800-880-3383 ext. 2, fax: 605-854-3064
  e-mail: info@liwms.com
  URL: *www.liwms.com*

- *The Little House Guidebook* by William Anderson and Leslie A. Kelly, HarperCollins, 1996. A guidebook to all the homes Laura Ingalls Wilder lived in that have been preserved as historic landmarks and museums. Includes site history and location information.

The Little Prince

Antoine de Saint-Exupery. Harcourt, 2000. ISBN: 0156012197

Age level: 9–12

About the book: A little prince from a small planet relates his adventures in seeking the secret of what is important in life.

Where you will travel: He pursues his inquiry through China; Turkey; France; New Zealand; Australia; Siberia; Russia; Indies; Africa; Europe; South America; North America; North Pole; South Pole; Arizona and the Sahara Desert.

For more information about China:

- Chinascape Web Index
  URL: *www.chinascape.org*

- Asia Voyages
  1650 Solano Ave., Suite A
  Berkeley, CA 94707
  tel: 800-914-9133, fax: 510-559-8863
  e-mail: info@asiavoyages.com
  URL: *www.asiavoyages.com*

For more information about Turkey:

- Learn more about Turkey
  URL: *www.about-turkey.com*

- Meander Adventures
  2029 Sidewinder Drive,
  P.O. Box 2730
  Park City, UT
  tel: 800-367-3230, fax: 435-649-1192
  URL: *www.meanderadventures.com*

For more information about France:

- The French Tourist Office
  URL: *www.francetourism.com/regionalin.htm*

For more information about New Zealand:

- The New Zealand Embassy
  37 Observatory Circle
  Washington DC 20008
  tel: 202-328-4800, fax: 202-667-5227
  e-mail: nz@nzemb.org
  URL: *www.nzemb.org*

For more information about Australia:

- AUS-info® Guides
  URL: *www.dcp.com.au/aus-info/aus/australia.html*

For more information about Russia and Siberia:

- The Russian National Tourist Office
  URL: *www.russia-travel.com*

- Library of Congress—Meeting of Frontiers
  URL: *http://frontiers.loc.gov/intldl/mtfhtml/mfsplash.html*

For more information about Africa:

- Columbia University's LibraryWeb—African Studies Internet Resources
  URL: *www.cc.columbia.edu/cu/libraries/indiv/area/Africa/index.html#ASIRcountry*

For more information about Europe:

- Visiteurope.com
  URL: *www.visiteurope.com*

For more information about South America:

- Encyclopedia.com—South America
  URL: *www.encyclopedia.com/articles/12112.html*

For more information about the Polar regions:

- Life on the Edge
  URL: *http://science.nasa.gov/newhome/headlines/msad13jan99_1.htm*

For more information about the Sahara Desert:

- Sahara Overland
  URL: *www.sahara-overland.com*

- Cnews—"Crossing the Empty Quarter" (story)
  URL: *www.canoe.ca/CNEWSFeatures9902/18_desert.html*

The Little Red Lighthouse and the Great Gray Bridge

Hildegarde H. Swift. Harcourt, 1974. ISBN: 0156528401

Age level: 3–6

About the book: The story of a little lighthouse who once ruled the river. It is unsure of its role as the great gray bridge is put over it, but finds it is still very much needed.

Where you will travel: The bridge is the George Washington Bridge in New York City. The lighthouse is in Fort Washington Park, 178th Street & Hudson River.

For more information about the Lighthouse and the George Washington Bridge:

- National Lighthouse Center and Museum—The Little Red Lighthouse
  URL: *www.lighthousemuseum.org/nylights/lred.html*

- New York City Urban Park Rangers
  1234 5th Ave.
  New York, NY 10029
  tel: 212-304-2365

Little Women

Louisa May Alcott. Penguin USA, 1997. ISBN: 0140380221

Age level: 11 and up

About the books: This classic book tells the story of the lives of the four March sisters—Meg, Jo, Beth and Amy—as they grow into young women in the mid-19th century. The characters are based on the Alcott family. *Little Men* and *Jo's Boys* continue the story of the life of the March family.

Where you will travel: The March family lived in Concord, Massachusetts. One sister moves to New York, New York and another to France.

For more information about the Alcotts:

- Orchard House
  P.O. Box 343
  Concord, MA 01742-0343
  tel: 978-369-4118
  URL: *www.louisamayalcott.org*

For more information about Concord, Massachusetts:

- Concordma.com
  URL: *www.concordma.com*

For more information about France:

- French Tourist Office
  URL: *www.francetourism.com/regionalin.htm*

For more information about New York:

- New York Convention & Visitors Bureau
  Visitor Information Center
  810 Seventh Ave.
  New York, NY 10019
  tel: 1-800-NYC-VISIT (U.S. and Canada) or 212-397-8222 (elsewhere)
  URL: *www.nycvisit.com*

The Lorax

Dr. Seuss. Random House, Inc., 1976. ISBN: 0394823370

Age level: 7–11

About the book: An old timer tells of a beautiful land that becomes industrialized despite the warnings of The Lorax. This story, about industrialism versus environmentalism, is presented in the manner of Dr. Seuss. It can be read aloud with children as young as five, but the depth of the meaning about protecting the environment makes it appropriate for older learners, too.

Where you will travel: Dr. Seuss looks at Weehawken, New Jersey and Lake Erie in New York and Canada.

For more information about Weehawken, New Jersey:

- Friends of the Weehawken Waterfront
  P.O. Box 5167
  Weehawken, NJ 07087
  tel: 201-223-1378
  e-mail: info@weehawkenwaterfront.com
  URL: *http://weehawkenwaterfront.com*

For more information about Lake Erie:

- Western Lake Erie Historical Society
  P.O. Box 5311
  Toledo, OH, 43611

- Bicycle Tour Books for Lake Erie
  Cyclotour Guide Books
  P.O. Box 10585
  Rochester, NY 1461
  tel: 716 244-6157
  e-mail: cyclotour@cyclotour.com

- Erie Quest Marine Heritage Area
  38 Erie St. N.
  Leamington, Ont. N8H 2Z3, Canada
  tel: 519-326-5761, ext. 236

- Lower Lakes Marine Historical Society
  66 Erie St.
  Buffalo, NY 14216
  tel: 716-849-0914

Loud Emily

Alexis O'Neill. Simon & Schuster, 1998. ISBN: 0689810784

Age level: 4–8

About the book: A little girl born in a whaling community in the nineteenth century has an unusually loud voice. She just can't find a place to be loud until she ventures onto a whaling ship.

Where you will travel: Emily's adventures take her to Baja, Mexico; Iceland; Cape Horn; New Bedford and Nantucket (island), Massachusetts; New London and Stonington, Connecticut and Sag Harbor, New York.

For more information about New Bedford and Nantucket Island, Massachusetts:

- New Bedford Whaling National Historical Park
  33 William St. or 37 North Second St.
  US Custom House
  New Bedford, MA 02740
  tel: 508-996-4469 or 508-996-4095
  New Bedford, MA 02740
  URL: *www.nps.gov/nebe/home.htm*

- The New Bedford Whaling Museum
  18 Johnny Cake Hill
  New Bedford, MA 02740-6398
  tel: 508-997-0046, fax: 508-997-0046
  URL: *http://whalingmuseum.org*

For more information about Stonington, Connecticut:

- The Town of Stonington, Connecticut
  URL: *www.munic.state.ct.us/STONINGTON/stonington.htm*

- MIS Coordinator
  Town of Stonington
  P.O. Box 352
  Stonington, CT 06378

For more information about Baja, Mexico:

- Baja Travel Guide
  URL: *www.bajatravel.com*

- Baja Expeditions
  2625 Garnet Ave.
  San Diego, CA 92109
  tel: 800-843-6967, fax: 858-581-6542
  e-mail: travel@bajaex.com

For more information about Iceland and Cape Horn:

- Islandia: A Guide to Iceland
  URL: *www.arctic.is/islandia*

Lyle, Lyle Crocodile

Bernard Waber. Houghton Mifflin, 1965. ISBN: 0395137209

Age level: 4–8

About the books: These delightful stories share the life of the Primm family who live in a house on "East 88th Street" in New York City and own a very refined crocodile as a pet. Other Lyle books are: *Lovable Lyle, Funny, Funny Lyle, Lyle Find His Mother, Lyle at the Office, Lyle and the Birthday Party,* and *Lyle at Christmas.*

Where you will travel: There is a neighborhood of brownstones on East 88th Street in New York City, New York.

For more information about New York:

- New York Convention & Visitors Bureau
  Visitor Information Center
  810 Seventh Ave.
  New York, NY 10019
  tel: 1-800-NYC-VISIT (U.S. and Canada) or 212-397-8222 (elsewhere)
  URL: *www.nycvisit.com*

Madeline

Ludwig Bemelmans. Penguin USA, 1969. ISBN: 0140501983

Age level: 4–8

About the books: Twelve girls live in Paris at a boarding school with their teacher Miss Clavel. One is petite but very brave, even when she has to go to the hospital in the middle of the night. Other Madeline books are: *Madeline and the Bad Hat, Madeline's Rescue, Madeline and the Gypsies, Madeline's Christmas, Madeline in London, Madeline in America.*

Where you will travel: The girls live in Paris, France and see the Eiffel Tower, the Opera House, Place Vendome, the Hotel Des Invalides, Notre Dame, the Luxembourg Gardens, the Church of the Sacre Coeur and the Tuileries Gardens facing the Louvre.

For more information about Paris:

- The Official Eiffel Tower Website—Virtual Tour
  URL: *www.tour-eiffel.fr/indexuk.html*

- GreatBuildings.com—Paris Opera House
  URL: *www.greatbuildings.com/cgi-bin/gbc-building.cgi/Paris_Opera.html*

- Paris.org—Hôtel National des Invalides
  URL: *www.paris.org/Musees/Invalides*

- The Louvre Museum
  URL: *www.louvre.fr/louvrea.htm*

- Columbia University's Notre-Dame Website
  URL: *www.learn.columbia.edu/notre-dame/index.html*

- Your Frenchconnexion.com
  URL: *www.yourfrenchconnexion.com/paris.html*

- Fodor's Gold Guides—Paris
  URL: *www.traveland.com.au/fg_e_Paris.asp*

Mailing May

Michael O. Tunnell. William Morrow & Co., 1997. ISBN: 0064437248

Age level: 5–9

About the book: Based on a true story, May's parents cannot afford a train ticket for her to visit her grandmother. Her father and uncle find a cheaper way to go by "mailing" her as a parcel through the United States Postal Service.

Where you will travel: She travels through Grangeville, Lewiston, Lapwai Canyon, Sweetwater and Joseph, Idaho.

For more information about the United States Postal Service:

- History of the U.S. Postal Service
  URL: *www.usps.gov/history/his1.htm*

For more information about Idaho:

- Scenic Idaho
  URL: *www.scenic-idaho.com*

- Images of Lapwai Canyon
  URL: *http://wallcloud.home.mindspring.com/grangevi.htm*

- Grangeville Chamber of Commerce
  P.O. Box 212
  Grangeville, ID 83501
  tel: 208-983-0460, fax: 208-983-1429
  URL: *www.grangevilleidaho.com*

- Lewiston, Idaho's Website
  URL: *www.lewiston.com*

Make Way for Ducklings

Robert McCloskey. Viking, 1976. ISBN: 0670451495

Age level: 3–6

About the book: A pair of ducks decides to raise a family in Boston. After a long walk through the streets of Boston, they decide to settle down in the Boston Public Garden.

Where you will travel: The mallards lived in Boston Public Garden, Boston, Massachusetts.

For more information about a tour of Mrs. Mallard's route:

- The Historic Neighborhoods Foundation
  99 Bedford St.
  Boston, MA 02111
  tel: 617-426-1885
  URL: *www.historic-neighborhoods.org*

For more information about Boston:

- Boston's official Website
  URL: *www.ci.boston.ma.us*

Mrs. Frisby and the Rats of NIMH

Robert C. O'Brien. Simon & Schuster, 1971. ISBN: 0689710682

Age level: 9–12

About the book: Mrs. Frisby, a widowed mouse with a sick child, is desperate and must turn to the exceptional rats living under the rosebush for help. There's something unusual and special about these rats.

Where you will travel: NIMH is the National Institute of Mental Health in Rockville, Maryland, just outside Washington, DC.

For more information about NIMH:

- NIMH Public Inquiries
  6001 Executive Blvd.
  Rm. 8184, MSC 9663
  Bethesda, MD 20892-9663
  tel: 301-443-4513, fax: 301-443-4279
  URL: *www.nimh.nih.gov/home.cfm*

Old Yeller

Fred Gipson. Harper Collins, 1976. ISBN: 006080971X

Age level: 9–12

About the book: This classic tells the story of a boy and his dog living in the Texas Hill Country in the 1800s. It is an account of a dog's loyalty to his adopted family with a poignant ending.

Where you will travel: The story takes place in Abilene, Kansas and San Antonio, Texas.

For more information about Abilene, Kansas:

- Abilene Area Chamber of Commerce
  URL: *www.abileneks.com/welcome.htm*

- Abilene Convention & Visitors Bureau
  201 NW 2nd
  Abilene, KS 67410
  tel: 800-569-5915

For more information about San Antonio, Texas:

- San Antonio Convention and Visitors Bureau
  P.O. Box 2277
  San Antonio, TX 78298-2277
  tel: 800-447-3372
  e-mail: sacvb@sanantoniocvb.com
  URL: *www.sanantoniocvb.com*

- The Handbook of Texas On-line
  URL: *www.tsha.utexas.edu/handbook/online/index.new.html*

Once a Pony Time at Chincoteague

Lynne N. Lockhart and Barbara M Lockhart. Cornell Maritime Press, 1992. ISBN: 0870334360

Age level: 6–9

About the book: An elderly couple takes a vacation to Chincoteague Island. There they enjoy the annual Pony Penning.

About pony penning on Chincoteague Island: There is an annual running of the horses in Chincoteague, and pony penning is held every year on the last Wednesday and Thursday of July.

Where you will travel: Chincoteague Island is off the coast of Virginia.

For more information about Chincoteague:

- Chincoteague Chamber of Commerce
  6733 Maddox Blvd.
  Chincoteague, VA 23336
  tel: 757-336-6161

- The Chincoteague Island Website
  URL: *www.chincoteague.com*

Oregon's Journey

Rascal. Troll, 1993. ISBN: 0816733066

Age level: 4–8

About the book: A clown helps a bear to leave the circus and find his home in the forest. The two achieve their goal after a long journey, including self-discovery.

Where you will travel: They travel through Pittsburgh, Pennsylvania; Chicago, Illinois; Iowa; the Great Plains; the Rocky Mountains and on to Oregon.

For more information about Pittsburgh, Pennsylvania:

- The Greater Pittsburgh Convention & Visitors Bureau
  tel: 800-359-0758
  URL: *www.pittsburgh-cvb.org*

For more information about Chicago, Illinois:

- The City of Chicago
  tel: 800-226-6632
  URL: *www.ci.chi.il.us*

For more information about Iowa:

- Iowa Division of Tourism
  Sioux City CVB
  801 4th St.
  Sioux City, IA 51102
  tel: 712-279-4800, fax: 712-279-4900

- Cedar Rapids CVB
  119 1st Ave., SE
  Cedar Rapids, IA 52401
  tel: 800-735-5557, fax: 319-398-5089

- Ames CVB
  213 Duff Ave.
  Ames, IA 50010
  tel: 800-288-7470, fax: 515-232-6716

For more information about the Great Plains:

- The Great Plains Nature Center
  6232 E 29th St.
  North, Wichita, KS 67220-2200
  tel: 316-683-5499, fax: 316-688-9555
  URL: *www.gpnc.org*

For more information about Rocky Mountain National Park:

- Rocky Mountain National Park
  URL: *www.nps.gov/romo*

For more information about Oregon:

- Welcome to Oregon.com
  URL: *www.el.com/to/oregon*

- The Oregon Tourism Commission
  tel: 800-547-7842
  e-mail: info.oregontourism@state.or.us
  URL: *www.traveloregon.com*

Paul Bunyan

Nanci A. Lyman. Troll, 1980. ISBN: 0893753106

Age level: 5–9

About the book: Paul Bunyan leads a remarkable life in this tall tale of the world's biggest, strongest lumberjack.

Where you will travel: This story says he was born in Maine and continues in the North Woods, "some say it was Minnesota or Michigan..." he dug the Great Lakes and worked in most of this country.

For more information about Paul Bunyan:

- Roadsideamerica.com—A Catalog of Bunyans
  URL: *www.roadsideamerica.com/set/bunylist.html*

For more information about Maine:

- Official Website of the State of Maine
  URL: *www.state.me.us*

- Maine Office of Tourism
  tel: 800-533-9595
  URL: *www.visitmaine.com*

For more information about the Paul Bunyan Trail in Minnesota:

- Paul Bunyan Trail
  URL: *www.paulbunyantrail.com*

For more information about Michigan and the Great Lakes:

- The Great Lakes Commission
  400 Fourth St., Argus II Bldg.
  Ann Arbor, MI 48103-4816
  tel: 734-665-9135, fax: 734-665-4370

Paul Revere's Ride

Henry Wadsworth Longfellow. Penguin USA, 1996. ISBN: 0140556125

Age level: 9–12

About the book: This famous poem recounts the historic ride of Paul Revere from Boston to Lexington and Concord to warn the colonists that the British were coming.

Where you will travel: Paul Revere rode from Boston to Concord and Lexington in Massachusetts.

For more information about Paul Revere:

- Paul Revere House
  URL: *www.paulreverehouse.org*

- The Minute Man National Historical Park
  URL: *www.nps.gov/mima*

For more information about Massachusetts:

- Massachusetts Office of Travel and Tourism
  URL: *www.massvacation.com*

Peter Pan

Sir James M. Barrie. Penguin USA, 1995. ISBN: 0140366741

Age level: 6–9

About the book: This is a classic story of childhood fantasies. With their magical friend Peter Pan, the Darling children, Wendy, John and Michael, find adventure in Never -Never Land.

Where you will travel: The family lives in London, England.

For more information about London:

- City of London's Website
  URL: *www.london.gov.uk*

- About.com—London
  URL: *http://london.about.com/mbody.htm*

A Picture Book of Sojourner Truth

David A. Adler. Holiday House, Inc., 1994. ISBN: 0823410722

Age level: 5–9

About the book: Along with pictures, this book is full of information about the life and many accomplishments of Sojourner Truth.

Where you will travel: Sojourner Truth was born a slave in Hurley, New York, she lived in Sing Sing (now Ossining) and New York City, New York, before she left to travel the United States preaching about religion, the rights of women and against slavery. During the Civil War she lived in Washington, D.C. She settled in Battle Creek, Michigan.

For more information about Sojourner Truth:

- The Sojourner Truth Institute
  5 Riverwalk Center, 34 W. Jackson St.
  Battle Creek, MI 49017
  tel: 616-965-2613, fax: 616-966-2495
  e-mail: Staff@SojournerTruth.org
  URL: *www.sojournertruth.org*

For more information about Hurley, New York:

- The Town Historian
  Town Hall,
  10 Wamsley Pl.
  P.O. Box 569
  Hurley, NY 12443
  e-mail at DBaker72@compuserve.com
  URL: *www.town.hurley.ny.us*

For more information about Ossining (Sing Sing), New York:

- The Town of Ossining
  URL: *www.townofossining.com*

- The Ossining Historical Society
  196 Croton Ave.
  Ossining, NY 10562
  tel: 914-941-0001

Pocahontas

Adapted by Gina Ingoglia. Disney Press, 1998. ISBN: 0786842164

Age level: 7–11

About the book: A retelling of the story of Pocahontas, the daughter of chief Powhatan, who befriended the white settlers from England, especially Captain John Smith.

Where you will travel: The story begins on the Virginia Coast of the Atlantic Ocean and continues in Jamestown and along the Chicahominy and Quiyoughcohannock Rivers, Virginia. Pocahontas travels to London, England and is presented to the Court.

For more information about Pocahontas:

- The Association for the Preservation of Virginia Antiquities—Pocahontas
  URL: *www.apva.org/history/pocahont.html*

For more information about Jamestown:

- Jamestown Rediscovery and Visitor Center
  Jamestown-Yorktown Foundation
  P.O. Box 1607
  Williamsburg, VA 23187
  tel: 888-593-4682

- The Association for the Preservation of Virginia Antiquities—Jamestown
  URL: *www.apva.org/history/index.html*

- Historynet.com—Jamestown
  URL: *www.historian.org/local/jamstwnva.htm*

For more information about London:

- City of London's Website
  URL: *www.london.gov.uk*

- About.com—London
  URL: *http://london.about.com/mbody.htm*

Ramona Quimby, Age 8

Beverly Cleary. Avon, 1992. ISBN: 0380709562

Age level: 7–11

About the books: This series of books is about Ramona and friends growing up in a suburb of Portland, Oregon. Other Ramona and Henry Huggins titles include *Ramona the Pest, Ramona the Brave, Ramona and her Father, Ramona and her Mother, Ramona Forever, Beezus and Ramona, Ribsy, Henry Huggins, Ramona's World, Henry and Ribsy, Henry and the Clubhouse, Henry and Beezus* and *Henry and the Paper Route.*

Where you will travel: The neighborhood is in the Grant Park neighborhood of Portland, Oregon. Klickitat Street is based on Hancock Street in Portland. There is a real Klickitat Street 2 blocks north of NE 37th Ave. NE 37th Ave. is where Beverly Bunn, now Beverly Cleary, grew up.

For more information about Beverly Cleary:

- The Multnomah County Library KidsPage—Beverly Cleary
  URL: *www.multnomah.lib.or.us/lib/kids/cleary.html*

For more information about Portland, Oregon:

- City of Portland
  URL: *www.ci.portland.or.us*

- The Portland Visitors Association
  1000 S.W. Broadway, Suite 2300
  Portland, OR 97205
  tel: 877-678-5263

- Portland Oregon Visitors Association
  URL: *www.pova.com/home/index.html*

- A Picture Tour of Multnomah County
  URL: *www.co.multnomah.or.us/about/tour0.html*

The Remarkable Ride of Israel Bissell

Alice Schick and Marjorie N. Allen. HarperCollins Children's Book Group, 1976. ISBN: 0397316763

Age level: 5–9

About the book: The illustrations help with humor to tell this true account of a post rider who rode on horseback to spread the word about the beginning of the American Revolutionary War.

Where you will travel: Israel Bissel travels through Lexington, Watertown, Waltham, Sudbury, Shrewsbury, Ware and Uxbridge, Massachusetts; Pomfret, Brooklyn, Plainfield, Norwich, New London, Lyme, Saybrook, Killingworth, Guilford, Branford, New Haven, Fairfield, Stamford, Mystic, Stratford, Norwalk and Horseneck, Connecticut; Rye and New York City, New York; Hackensack, Passaic, Newark, New Brunswick, Princeton and Trenton, New Jersey; Philadelphia, Pennsylvania and Georgia.

For more information about the Revolutionary War:

- Cyber Haus—A Revolutionary Day along Historical US Route 4
  159 Delaware Ave.
  Delmar, NY 12054
  URL: *www.cyhaus.com/usroute4/default.htm*

- New Jersey During The Revolution
  URL: *http://njrev.20m.com/NJ/index.html*

- New Jersey Department of Environmental Protection
  Division of Science, Technology and Research
  29 Arctic Parkway,
  P.O. Box 427
  Trenton, NJ 08625
  tel: 609-292-1185

- Connecticut Society of the Sons of the American Revolution
  158 Meadowview Dr.
  Torrington, CT 06790
  tel: 860-482-6895
  e-mail: ussmo@aol.com
  URL: *www.societyct.org/ctssar.htm*

- Sons of the Revolution of the State of California—Information on Uniforms
  URL: *www.walika.com/sr/uniforms/p6.htm*

- Boston National Historical Park
  Charlestown Navy Yard
  Boston, MA 02129-4543
  tel: 617-242-564, fax 617-242-6006
  e-mail: Bost_Email@nps.gov
  URL: *www.nps.gov/bost*

A River Ran Wild

Lynne Cherry. Houghton Mifflin College, 1995. ISBN: 0395732409

Age level: 5–9

About the book: When native people first settled on the banks of the river now called the Nashua, it was a fertile and beautiful place. The story follows the river through time as it becomes polluted and then restored through the efforts of Marion Stoddart and the Nashua River Watershed Association.

Where you will travel: The Nashua River runs through New Hampshire and Massachusetts.

For more information about the Nashua River:

- Nashua River Watershed Association
  592 Main St.
  Groton, MA 01450
  tel: 978-448-0299, fax: 978-448-0941
  e-mail: nrwa@ma.ultranet.com
  URL: *www.ultranet.com/~nrwa*

Ruby Mae

David Small. Crown Publishers, 1992. ISBN-0-517-58248-1

Age level: 6–9

About the book: A woman gets nervous speaking in public until her nephew saves the day with his invention. But when she is invited to speak before the UN, her "hat" is stolen. The nephew creates a solution so that Aunt Ruby can deliver a message for world peace.

Where you will travel: Nada, Texas, can be found in Colorado County, which is part of South Central Texas. The United Nations is located in New York City, New York.

For more information about Texas:

- TexasEscapes.com
  URL: *www.texasescapes.com*

For more information about the United Nations:

- United Nations
  URL: *www.un.org* (for information)
  URL: *www.un.org/Pubs/CyberSchoolBus* (for a virtual tour)

Sarah, Plain and Tall

Patricia Mac Lachlan. Harper Collins, 1987. ISBN: 0064402053

Age level: 9–12

About the book: Sarah answers an advertisement for a bride from a Kansas widower with two children. Although Sarah is homesick for her home in Maine, she grows to love the two youngsters and their father on the prairie farm. She shows them the beauty of Maine through her illustrations, and they show her the beauty of the prairie.

Where you will travel: Sarah moved from Maine's coastland to a farm on the Kansas prairie.

For more information about the book's setting:

- University of Texas—Sarah, Plain and Tall
  URL: *www.gslis.utexas.edu/~schapa/page.html*

For more information about Maine:

- Maine Office of Tourism
  tel: 888-624-6345
  URL: *www.visitmaine.com*

- Bi-National Quoddy Loop
  URL: *www.quoddyloop.com*

For more information about Kansas:

- State of Kansas
  URL: *www.accesskansas.org*

- Kansas State Historical Society
  6425 SW Sixth Ave.
  Topeka, KS 66615-1099
  tel: 785-272-8681, TTY 785272-8683
  URL: *www.kshs.org/index.htm*

For more information about the prairie:

- Prairie Expo
  URL: *www.prairie-expo.com*

Shaker Boy

Mary Lyn Ray . Harcourt Brace & Company, 1994. ISBN: 0152769218

Age level: 6–9

About the book: At the age of 6 years old, Caleb's life changes because his father dies in the Civil War and his mom sends him away. Caleb begins a new life as part of the Shaker Community.

Where you will travel: The Shaker Community is in Canterbury, New Hampshire. Mills were located primarily in New England and in New York and New Jersey.

For more information about Shakers:

- Canterbury Shaker Community
  288 Shaker Rd.
  Canterbury, NH 03224
  tel: 800-982-9511
  URL: *www.shakers.org*

- The Shaker Museum
  707 Shaker Rd.
  New Gloucester, ME 04260
  tel: 207-926-4597
  URL: *www.shakerworkshops.com/sdl.htm*

For more information about Lake Winnipesaukee, New Hampshire:

- Lake Winnipesaukee
  URL: *www.winnipesaukee.com*

- WeirsCam.com—Live Images of Lake Winnipesaukee
  URL: *http://winnipesaukee.com/weirscam*

For more information about maple syrup:

- Thatcher's Sugarhouse
  12 Broom St.
  Plainfield, MA 01070
  tel: 413-634-5582, fax: 413-634-5582
  URL: *www.bcn.net/~thatcher/index.htm*

For more information about Lowell, Massachusetts mills:

- The Lowell Historical Society
  Boott Cotton Mills Museum
  400 Foot of John St., Fourth Floor
  Lowell, MA 01853
  tel: 978-970-5180
  URL: *www.uml.edu/community/lhs*

- University of Massachusetts Lowell Libraries
  Center for Lowell History
  Patrick J. Mogan Cultural Center
  40 French St.
  Lowell, MA 01852
  tel: 978-934-4997, fax: 978-934-4995
  URL: *http://libweb.uml.edu/clh/index.Html*

Sign of the Beaver

Elizabeth George Speare. Dell, 1983. ISBN: 0440479002

Age level: 10–12

About the book: A 12-year-old colonial boy is left alone in the Maine woods near the Penobscot River to look after the family homestead while his father goes back to Massachusetts to get the rest of the family. The boy learns of friendship and survival from the local Native Americans.

Where you will travel: The story takes place in the Bangor and Orono, Maine, area as the family moves from Massachusetts.

For more information about Acadia National Park:

- Acadia National Park Old Town
  P.O. Box 177,
  Eagle Lake Rd.
  Bar Harbor, ME 04609-0177
  tel: 207-288-3338, fax: 207-288-5507
  e-mail: Acadia_Information@nps.gov
  URL: *www.nps.gov/acad*

For more information about Native Americans of the Northeast:

- Hudson Museum at the University of Maine
  5746 Maine Center for the Arts
  Orono, ME 04469-5746
  tel: 207-581-1901
  e-mail: hudsonmuseum@umit.maine.edu
  URL: *www.umaine.edu/hudsonmuseum*

A Small Tall Tale from the Far Far North

Peter Sîs. Farrar, Straus & Giroux, NY, 1993. ISBN: 0374467250

Age level: 7–10

About the book: Jan Welzl, a Czech folk hero, traveled 100 years ago through the Arctic and Alaska. He was helped and befriended by the Eskimos who lived there. They taught him how to survive the harsh climate, and in return he was able to help protect them from gold diggers. The book is based on the real experiences of Welzl, who spent 30 years in this frozen land.

Where you will travel: Jan Welzl left the Czech Republic (then part of Czechoslovakia) and traveled across Russia, through Siberia, to the Bering Sea and St. Lawrence Island, Alaska.

For more information about Czechoslovakia and the Czech Republic:

- Learning Network's InfoPlease—Czechoslovakia
  URL: *www.infoplease.com/ce6/world/A0814445.html*

For more information about Russia's Trans-Siberian Railway:

- Interknowledge—Trans-Siberian Railway
  URL: *www.interknowledge.com/russia/trasib01.htm*

For more information about the Bering Sea and North Pacific Ocean:

- National Oceanic and Atmospheric Administration—Bering Sea
  URL: *www.pmel.noaa.gov/bering*

For more information about Alaska and Eskimos:

- State of Alaska Tourism Website
  URL: *www.travelalaska.com/homepage.html*

- Encyclopedia.com— Eskimo
  URL: *www.encyclopedia.com/articles/04219.html*

- Agayuliyararput—Native Alaskan Yup'ik material presented from a Yup'ik perspective
  URL: *www.mnh.si.edu/arctic/features/yupik*

Snowflake Bentley

Jacqueline Briggs Martin. Houghton Mifflin Company, 1998. ISBN: 0395861624

Age level: 5–9

About the book: Wilson A. Bentley always loved the snow. He used photography to study snowflakes and discovered, among other things, the fact that no two snowflakes are alike.

Where you will travel: Bentley lived in Jericho, Vermont. Vermont's Lake Champlain and Mount Mansfield are also in the book.

For more information about Wilson Bentley and Jericho, Vermont:

- Jericho Historical Society
  P.O. Box 35
  Jericho, VT 05465
  e-mail: info@snowflakebentley.com
  URL: *www.snowflakebentley.com*

- Lake Champlain Regional Marketing Organization
  60 Main St., Suite 100
  Burligton, VT 05401
  tel: 802-863-3489, fax: 802- 863-1538
  e-mail: vermont@vermont.org
  URL: *www.vermont.org*

- Virtual Vermont Internet Magazine
  URL: *www.virtualvermont.com*

The Story About Ping

Marjorie Flack and Kurt Wiese. Penguin Putnam Books for Young Readers, 1971.
ISBN: 0140502416

Age level: 4–8

About the book: Ping is a little duck who lives on the Yangtze River. As he travels along the river he is often tardy getting home.

Where you will travel: Yangtze River and the town of Guilin on the Lee River in China are the places Ping sees.

For more information about China:

- Chinascape Web Index
  URL: *www.chinascape.org*

- Asia Voyages
  1650 Solano Ave., Suite A
  Berkeley, CA 94707
  tel: 800-914-9133, fax: 510-559-8863
  e-mail: info@asiavoyages.com
  URL: *asiavoyages.com*

- Yangtze River Tour
  URL: *www.chinavista.com/travel/yangtze/main.html*

Strega Nona: An Old Tale

Tomie de Paola. Simon & Schuster Children's, 1975. ISBN: 0671666061

Age level: 4–8

About the books: Big Anthony works for Strega Nona (Grandmother Witch) who lives outside of the town of Calabria, Italy and helps the townspeople with their problems. One day Strega Nona goes out and warns Big Anthony not to touch her magic pasta pot. Of course Big Anthony does touch the pot and everyone finds out about it. Other Strega Nona books are *Strega Nona Takes a Vacation, Merry Christmas Strega Nona, Strega Nona: Her Story, Strega Nona Meets Her Match, Strega Nona's Magic Lessons.*

Where you will travel: The town Reggio di Calabria is in the region of Italy called Calabria and located at the tip of the Italian peninsula.

For more information about Italian:

- About.com's—Italian for Children
  URL: *http://italian.about.com/library/children/blchildrenhome.htm*

For more information about Italy:

- Italy Cyber Guide
  URL: *www.italycyberguide.com*

- Italian Government Tourist Board
  URL: *www.italiantourism.com*

- Italian Offices of Tourism in the U.S
  630 Fifth Ave., Suite 1565
  New York, NY 10111
  tel: 212-245-5618, fax: 212-586-9249

  500 North Michigan Ave., Suite 2240
  Chicago, IL 60611
  tel: 312-644-0996, fax: 312-644-3019

  12400 Wilshire Blvd., Suite 550
  Los Angeles, CA 90025
  tel: 310-820-1898, fax: 310-820-6357

- Windows on Italy
  URL: *www.mi.cnr.it/WOI*
  Choose "Regions," then choose "Calabria" for pictures of the Calabria region.

Stuart Little

E.B. White. HarperCollins Children's Books, 1974. ISBN: 0064400565

Age level: 8–10

About the book: A New York City family with one son adopts another son who happens to be a mouse. This is charming story about the adventures of a mouse trying to live as a boy. Among other adventures, Stuart Little sails a remote-control boat across the lake in Central Park.

Where you will travel: The family visits various locales in New York City, New York.

For more information about New York:

- New York Convention & Visitors Bureau
  Visitor Information Center
  810 Seventh Ave.
  New York, NY 10019
  tel: 1-800-NYC-VISIT (U.S. and Canada) or 212-397-8222 (elsewhere)
  URL: *www.nycvisit.com*

Take Me out to the Ballgame

Jack Norworth. Simon & Schuster Children's, 1999. ISBN: 0689824335

Age level: 4–8

About the book: This classic baseball song is illustrated with scenes from the fifth game of the 1947 World Series. A great book for a sing-a-long.

Where you will travel: The games between the two New York teams (Yankees and Mets) were played at Yankee Stadium in the Bronx and Ebbets Field (no longer standing) in Brooklyn, both in New York City.

For more information about sports history and stadiums:

- Hickoksports.com's History Web Page
  URL: *www.hickoksports.com/history/worldser.shtml*

- Ballparks.com—Ebbets Field
  URL: *www.ballparks.com/baseball/national/ebbets.htm*

- Ballparks.com—Yankee Stadium
  URL: *www.ballparks.com/baseball/american/yankee.htm*

- The Office Website for Major League Baseball
  URL: *www.mlb.com*

For more information about New York:

- New York Convention & Visitors Bureau
  Visitor Information Center
  810 Seventh Ave.
  New York, NY 10019
  tel: 1-800-NYC-VISIT (U.S. and Canada) or 212-397-8222 (elsewhere)
  URL: *www.nycvisit.com*

Tar Beach

Faith Ringgold. Crown Publishing Group, 1996. ISBN: 0517885441

Age level: 6–9

About the book: A young girl takes charge of her world as she "flies" over her neighborhood from her tar rooftop in Harlem. "Fly" along with the girl and her brother in this allegorical tale that sparkles with symbolic and historical references to African-American culture in Harlem during 1939.

Where you will travel: Harlem is in Manhattan, a borough of New York, New York, bordering the Hudson River near the George Washington Bridge.

For more information about Harlem:

- Home to Harlem
  URL: *www.HOMETOHARLEM.COM*

- Welcome to East Harlem On-line
  URL: *www.east-harlem.com*

- Harlem: Mecca of the New Negro
  URL: *http://etext.lib.virginia.edu/harlem*

For more information about the George Washington Bridge:

- Port Athority of New York and New Jersey's George Washington Bridge
  URL: *www.panynj.gov/tbt/gwmain.HTM*

- Hudson River Museum
  tel: 914-963-4550 ext. 212
  URL: *www.hrm.org*

This Land Is Your Land

Words and music by Woody Guthrie, with a tribute by Pete Seeger. Little, Brown & Company, 1998. ISBN: 0316392154

Age level: 5–9

About the book: The ballad as a book takes the reader on a walk from coast to coast, with notations and illustrations to provide details. Children of all ages can sing, read and perform this book for an audience of peers, parents and invited guests.

Where you will travel: The book and song move around the United States: the Golden Gate Bridge, San Francisco, California; Gulf Stream Waters; Redwood Forests; Hollywood Hills; Niagara Falls; Brooklyn Bridge, New York; the Empire State Building, New York; Statue of Liberty, Liberty State Park, New Jersey; Battery Park, New York; New York Island, New York; Iowa cornfields; Gulf of Mexico; Pampa, Texas; Mardi Gras, New Orleans; Mississippi River; Gateway Arch, St. Louis, Missouri; Los Angeles City Hall; Okemah, Oklahoma; Water Tower, Chicago, Illinois; Yellowstone National Park; Yosemite National Park; Grand Coulee Dam; Diamond Head and Waikiki Beach Honolulu; Coney Island Amusement Park; Washington Monument; Crazy Horse Memorial, South Dakota; Mount Rushmore, South Dakota; Stone Mountain Memorial, Georgia; Seattle Space Needle; Firestone Farm in Greenfield Village, Michigan; Portland Head Light Station, Maine; Mesa Verde, Colorado; Oak Alley, Vacherie, Louisiana; Brooks Range, Alaska; Space Shuttle launch, Florida; Watts Towers in Los Angeles; Boston Pops in Boston Harbor; a totem pole in Ketchikan, Alaska; Cleveland, Ohio; the Pacific coast of California.

For more information about America's cities:

- Your Link To America's Cities
  URL: *www.usacitylink.com/citylink*

- US State Travel Department
  URL: *www.bcpl.net/~mcohn/statelnk.htm*

For more information about National Parks:

- National Park Service
  1849 C St. NW
  Washington, DC 20240
  tel: 202 208-6843
  URL: *www.nps.gov*

Through My Eyes

Ruby Bridges. Scholastic, Inc., 1999. ISBN: 0590189239

Age level: 7–11

About the book: This is the story of Ruby Bridges, the first black child to attend the all-white William Frantz Public School in New Orleans, Louisiana. Her courage opened the door for others to follow and signaled a change in this nation.

Where you will travel: Locations mentioned in the book are Storyland at City Park in New Orleans, Louisiana; Baton Rouge, Louisiana; Tylertown and Jackson, Mississippi; Little Rock, Arkansas; Boston, Massachusetts; Washington, DC; Montgomery, Alabama; Greensboro, North Carolina and Memphis, Tennessee.

For more information about Ruby Bridges:

- NewsHour— A Class Of One
  URL: *www.pbs.org/newshour/bb/race_relations/jan-june97/bridges_2-18.html*

- Utah University's TeacherLink—Lesson Plan for Ruby Bridges
  URL: *http://teacherlink.ed.usu.edu/TLresources/longterm/LessonPlans/famous/rubybrid.html*

For more information about New Orleans, Louisiana:

- Storyland in New Orleans City Park
  1 Palm Dr.
  New Orleans, LA 70124-4600
  tel: 504-482-4888
  URL: *www.mardi.com/index_s.htm*

For more information about Tylertown, Mississippi:

- Walthall County Chamber of Commerce
  URL: *www.walthallcountychamber.org*

For more information about Montgomery, Alabama:

- The City of Montgomery
  P.O. Box 1111
  Montgomery, AL 36101-1111
  tel: 334-241-2200
  URL: *http://montgomery.al.us*

For more information about Greensboro, North Carolina:

- The City of Greensboro
  URL: *www.ci.greensboro.nc.us*

For more information about Memphis, Tennessee:

- City of Memphis
  URL: *www.ci.memphis.tn.us/visitor_info/main.cfm*

For more information about integrated education and Civil Rights:

- Tri-State Education Initiative Educator Resource Center
  P.O. Box 508
  Iuka, MS 38852
  tel: 601-423-7454, fax: 601-423-7458
  e-mail: webmaster@edubbs.tsei.k12.ms.us

- Historic Places of the Civil Rights Movement
  URL: *www.cr.nps.gov/nr/travel/civilrights/index.htm*

Tikvah Means Hope

Patricia Polacco. Doubleday Dell Books for Young Readers, 1996. ISBN: 0440412293

Age level: 4–8

About the book: A fire destroys much of the property in a community. However, a cat restores their faith in the goodness of neighbors and hope for the future.

Where you will travel: The community of people is in Oakland, California.

For more information about Oakland, California:

- The City of Oakland
  URL: www.oaklandnet.com

- Photos of Oakland, California
  URL: *www.crosswinds.net/~transitguide/photos/oakland1.htm*

Train Song

Diane Siebert. HarperCollins Children's Books, 1993. ISBN: 0064433404

Age level: 4–8

About the book: Celebrate a love of all types of trains and enjoy the railroad trip from New York, New York to Seattle, Washington.

Where you will travel: The train travels through New York City and Buffalo, New York; Boston, Massachusetts; North Platte, Nebraska; Dallas, Fort Worth and Abilene, Texas; Los Angeles, California; Santa Fe, New Mexico and to Seattle, Washington.

For more information about traveling cross-country:

- NY 2 LA
  URL: *http://owls.tuj.ac.jp/~heimbach/NY2LA/index.html*
  An action maze where travelers move from state to state by naming the capital of each state they'd like to visit.

For more information about rail travel:

- Association of Rail Travel in the U.S.
  URL: *www.ustraintravel.com*

- Amtrak
  tel: 800-872-7245
  URL: *www.amtrak.com*

- General Director of Public Affairs
  Burlington Northern Santa Fe
  tel: 913-551-4479, fax: 913-551-4285

For more information about Buffalo, New York:

- Buffalo Niagara Convention & Visitors Bureau
  617 Main St., Suite 400
  Buffalo, NY 14203-1496
  tel: 888-2BUFFNY
  e-mail: info@buffalocvb.org
  URL: *www.buffalocvb.org/home.html*

For more information about Abilene, Texas:

- City of Abilene
  URL: *www.abilene.com*

- Texas.com
  URL: *www.texas.com*

For more information about Santa Fe, New Mexico:

- City of Santa Fe
  URL: *http://sfweb.ci.santa-fe.nm.us*

- Santa Fe Convention and Visitors Bureau
  URL: *www.santafe.org*

Traveling to Tondo

Verna Aardema. Alfred A. Knopf, 1994. ISBN: 067985309X

Age level: 6–9

About the book: This delightful African folktale is the story of four foolish friends: a pigeon, a python, a tortoise and a civet cat. They are traveling to the civet cat's wedding in Tondo, Democratic Republic of Congo, when they decide to wait for one another, no matter how long it takes.

Where you will travel: They travel within the Democratic Republic of Congo (formerly Zaire, sometimes referred to as the Congo—Kinshasa).

For more information about the Democratic Republic of Congo:

- Democratic Republic of Congo—Factsheet
  URL: *www.rnw.nl/foreign/popup/html/popup_congo991118.html*

- Congo Pages
  URL: *www.congo-pages.org/welcome.htm*

26 Fairmount Avenue

Tomie dePaola. Puffin, 2001. ISBN: 0698118642

Age level: 6–9

About the book: Spend a year with Tomie dePaola and his family as they prepare to move from an apartment into a new house.

Where you will travel: You visit 26 Fairmount Avenue in Meriden, Connecticut; Columbus Avenue, Meriden, Connecticut; Wallingford, Connecticut; Yalesville, Connecticut; Tracy, Connecticut; South Meriden, Connecticut; Bronx, New York; Times Square, New York City; Fall River, Massachusetts.

For more information about Connecticut:

- Historic Connecticut
  URL: *www.tourism.state.ct.us/qtrips/historic.htm*

- For a free Connecticut Vacation Kit, call
  Connecticut Vacation Center
  1-800-CT BOUND (1-800-282-6863)

For more information about the Bronx in New York:

- BronxPress.com
  URL: *www.bronx.com*

- Greetings from the Bronx, New York
  URL: *http://bronxnewyork.com*

- The Bronx County Historical Society
  3309 Bainbridge Ave.
  The Bronx, NY 10467
  tel: 718-881-8900, fax: 718-881-4827

- New York Convention & Visitors Bureau
  Visitor Information Center
  810 Seventh Ave.
  New York, NY 10019
  tel: 1-800-NYC-VISIT (U.S. and Canada) or 212-397-8222 (elsewhere)
  URL: *www.nycvisit.com*

For more information about Battleship Cove, Fall River, Massachusetts:

- Battleship Massachusetts
  tel: 508-678-1100
  URL: *www.battleshipcove.com*

Wanted Dead or Alive: The True Story of Harriet Tubman

Ann McGovern. Scholastic, Inc., 1991. ISBN: 0590442120

Age level: 7–11

About the book: This is the story of the remarkable life of Harriet Tubman. She was born a slave on a Maryland plantation and eventually led 300 slaves to freedom.

Where you will travel: The story covers Maryland, Pennsylvania, New York and Canada.

For more information about Harriet Tubman:

- The Birthplace of Harriet Tubman
  Green Briar Rd.
  Cambridge, MD 21613
  tel: 410-228-0401

- The Harriet Tubman Museum and Gift Shop
  424 Race St.
  Cambridge, MD 21613
  tel: 410-228-0401

- The Harriet Tubman Home
  180 South St.
  Auburn, NY 13201
  tel: 315-252-2081
  e-mail: HTHome@localnet.com
  URL: *www.nyhistory.com/harriettubman/index.htm*

For more information about the Underground Railroad:

- National Geographic—Underground Railroad
  URL: *www.nationalgeographic.com/railroad/index.html*

- African Canadian Heritage Tour
  URL: *www.ciaccess.com/~jdnewby/heritage/african.htm*

For more information about the American South:

- University of North Carolina's American South
  URL: *http://docsouth.unc.edu/index.html*

For more information about Pennsylvania:

- Pennsylvania's Official Website
  URL: *www.state.pa.us*

- Pennsylvania Travel and Tourism Office
  tel: 800-847-4872

For more information about Maryland:

- Maryland's African-American Heritage Website
  URL: *http://library.thinkquest.org/10854*

- Maryland Division of Tourism, Film and the Arts
  217 East Redwood St., 9th Floor
  Baltimore, MD 21202
  tel: 800-634-7386
  URL: *www.mdisfun.org*

The West Texas Chili Monster

Judy Cox. BridgeWater Books, 1998. ISBN: 0816745463

Age level: 5–9

About the book: A family encourages Mama to enter the chili tasting contest. But, just as the judges are getting ready to taste her chili, the food disappears.

Where you will travel: The book moves from west Texas to the lobster coasts of Maine, the "rainy" plains of Spain and Mississippi.

For more information about Texas:

- Texas.com
  URL: *www.texas.com*

- Texas Historical Commission
  P.O. Box 12276
  Austin, TX 78711-2276
  tel: 512-463-6100, fax: 512-475-4872
  e-mail: thc@thc.state.tx.us.

For more information about Maine lobster:

- Maine Lobster Promotion Council
  382 Harlow St.
  Bangor, ME, 04401
  tel: 207-947-2966
  e-mail: info@mainelobsterpromo.com
  URL: *www.mainelobsterpromo.com*

For more information about the effects of the lack of rain in Spain:

- Birding in Spain
  URL: *www.spruceroots.org/Birds/Spain.html*

For more information about Mississippi:

- Mississippi Development Authority Division of Tourism Development
  P.O. Box 849
  Jackson, MS 39205
  tel: 601-359-3297, fax: 601-359-5757
  URL: *www.visitmississippi.org/resources/index.htm*

Where is Grandpa?

T. A. Barron. The Putnam Publishing Group, 1999. ISBN: 0399230378

Age level: 5–9

About the book: A boy misses his beloved grandpa and asks the title question to his family. With the help of his father, the boy comes to realize that his grandpa will always be near.

Where you will travel: Locations include the Never Summer Range of the Rocky Mountains; the Salmon River in Vancouver, British Columbia, Canada and the Connecticut River in Essex, Connecticut.

For more information about the Rocky Mountains:

- Encyclopedia.com—Rocky Mountains
  url: *www.encyclopedia.com/articles/11062.html*

- Rocky Mountain National Park
  url: *www.nps.gov/romo/index.htm*

For more information about the Salmon River:

- BCAdventure.com—Salmon River
  url: *www.bcadventure.com/adventure/angling/protalk/thornton/salmon/river.phtml*

For more information about the Connecticut River:

- Connecticut River Museum
  67 Main St.
  Essex, CT 06426
  tel: 860-767-8269, fax: 860-767-7028
  url: *www.ctrivermuseum.org*

William Shakespeare and the Globe

Aliki. HarperCollins Children's Books, 2000. ISBN: 0064437221

Age level: 5–9

About the book: This book tells the life story of William Shakespeare and gives a history lesson about the Globe Theater. The author opens up the world of Shakespeare and the Globe Theatre to children and teachers.

Where you will travel: The London locations in the book are Shakespeare's Globe, Bankside Walk, St. Mary Overies/Southwark Cathedral, St. Paul's Cathedral, Tower of London and George Inn. In Stratford-Upon-Avon, they are Henley Street, Anne Hathaway's Cottage, Shottery, Mary Arden's House, Wilmcote, Gardens in site of New Place, Guild Church and Grammar School, Holy Trinity Church and Clopton Bridge.

For more information about Shakespeare:

- The Shakespeare Resource Center
  url: *www.bardweb.net*

- Shakespeare's Globe Theater
  url: *www.shakespeares-globe.org*

- GlobeLink
  Shakespeare's Globe
  New Globe Walk,
  London SE1 9DT
  United Kingdom
  tel: + 44-20-7401-9919, fax +44-20-7902-1475

- The Shakespeare's Stratford Website
  url: *www.stratford.co.uk*

- Shakespeare's Birthplace and Properties
  url: *www.stratford.co.uk/birthplace/home.html*

- Stratford-upon-Avon Tourist Information Center
  Bridgefoot
  Stratford-upon-Avon CV37 6GW
  United Kingdom
  tel: +44 1789 293 127
  url: *www.stratford-upon-avon.co.uk*

- Warwick Tourist Information Center
  Court House
  Jury Street
  Warwick CV34 4EW
  United Kindom
  tel: +44 1926 492 212
  url: *www.warwick-uk.co.uk*

A Witch Got on at Paddington Station

Dyan Sheldon. E. P. Dutton, 1987. ISBN: 0525443525

Age level: 5–9

About the book: On a rainy London day, the bus is crowded. The day becomes full of fun when a witch gets on board.

Where you will travel: The bus is in London, the United Kingdom, at Paddington Station and Victoria Station.

For more information about London:

- City of London
  url: *www.london.gov.uk*

- About.com—London
  url: *http://london.about.com/mbody.htm*

For more information about Paddington Station and Victoria Station:

- University of Reading—Paddington Station
  url: *www.rdg.ac.uk/~esu98dhs/htm/station.htm*

- Explore-London's Victoria Station
  url: *www.explore-london.co.uk/vicst1.html*

- University of Reading—Paddington Bear Web Page
  url: *www.rdg.ac.uk/~esu98dhs/htm/paddinton.htm*

Zachary's Ball

Matt Tavares. Candlewick Press, 2000. ISBN: 0763607304

Age level: 7–11

About the book: Zachary's father takes him to a Boston Red Sox baseball game at Fenway Park. When his father catches a ball and hands it to Zachary, something magical happens.

Where you will travel: Fenway Park in Boston, Massachusetts is the setting for this story.

For more information about Boston:

- Boston's Official Website
  url: *www.ci.boston.ma.us*

For more information about Fenway Park:

- The Boston Red Sox Website
  url: *http://redsox.mlb.com/NASApp/mlb/bos/homepage/bos_homepage.jsp*
  Click on "Fenway Park."

Appendix A
Books by Read-aloud Age

3-6 years old
Blueberries for Sal by Robert McCloskey
The Little Red Lighthouse and the Great Gray Bridge by Hildegarde H. Swift
Make Way for Ducklings by Robert McCloskey

4-8 year old
Amelia and Eleanor Go for a Ride by Pam Muñoz Ryan
Arthur Meets the President by Marc Brown
Chicken Soup With Rice by M. Sendak
Horton Hatches the Egg by Dr. Seuss
Huckabuck Family and How They Raised Popcorn in Nebraska and Quit and Came Back by Carl Sandburg
Loud Emily by Alexis O'Neill
Lyle, Lyle Crocodile by Bernard Waber
Madeline by Ludwig Bemelmans
Oregon's Journey by Rascal
The Story About Ping by Marjorie Flack and Kurt Wiese
Strega Nona: An Old Tale by Tomie de Paola
Take Me Out to the Ballgame by Jack Norworth
Tikvah Means Hope by Patricia Polacco
Train Song by Diane Siebert

5-9 year olds
Abuela by Arthur Dorros
Aunt Flossie's Hats (and Crab Cakes Later) by Elizabeth Fitzgerald Howard
The Ballot Box Battle by Emily Arnold
Bloomers! by Rhoda Blumberg
The Fiddler of the Northern Lights by Natalie Kinsey-Warnock
Hannah and the Whistling Teakettle by Mindy Warshaw Skolsky
Jambo Means Hello: Swahili Alphabet Book by Muriel Feelings
Journey to Freedom by Courtni C. Wright
Mailing May by Michael O. Tunnell
Paul Bunyan by Nanci A. Lyman
A Picture Book of Sojourner Truth by David A. Adler
The Remarkable Ride of Israel Bissell by Alice Schick and Marjorie N. Allen
A River Ran Wild by Lynne Cherry
Snowflake Bentley by Jacqueline Briggs Martin
This Land Is Your Land, words and music by Woody Guthrie, with a tribute by Pete Seeger
The West Texas Chili Monster by Judy Cox
Where is Grandpa? by T. A. Barron
William Shakespeare and the Globe by Aliki
A Witch Got on at Paddington Station by Dyan Sheldon

6-9 year olds
The Absolutely Essential Eloise by Kay Thompson
American Girl Series by Pleasant Company
Beautiful Warrior: The Legend of the Nun's Kung Fu by Emily Arnold McCully
The Biggest and the Best Flag That Ever Flew by Rebecca C. Jones

Bingleman's Midway by Karen Ackerman
Casey Jones' Fireman: The Story of Sim Webb by Nancy Farmer
The Fortune Tellers by Lloyd Alexander
How to Make Apple Pie and See the World by Marjorie Priceman
Once a Pony Time at Chincoteague by Lynne N. Lockhart and Barbara M Lockhart
Peter Pan by Sir James M. Barrie
Ruby Mae by David Small
Shaker Boy by Mary Lyn Ray
Tar Beach by Faith Ringgold
Traveling to Tondo by Verna Aardema
26 Fairmount Avenue by Tomie dePaola

7-11 year olds
The Bracelet by Yoshiko Uchida
The Boston Coffee Party by Doreen Rappaport
The Lorax by Dr. Seuss
Pocahontas by Disney
Ramona Quimby, Age 8 by Beverly Cleary
A Small Tall Tale from the Far Far North by Peter Sis
Through My Eyes by Ruby Bridges
Zachary's Ball by Matt Tavares

8-12 year olds
All-of-a-Kind-Family by Sydney Taylor
And Then What Happened, Paul Revere? by Jean Fritz
Ben and Me: An Astonishing Life of Benjamin Franklin as Written by His Good Mouse Amos by Robert Lawson
Caddie Woodlawn by Carol Ryrie Brink
In the Year of the Boar and Jackie Robinson by Bette Bao Lord
Little House on the Prairie by Laura Ingalls Wilder
Stuart Little by E.B. White

9-12 year olds
Baseball Saved Us by Ken Mochizuki
From the Mixed Up Files of Mrs. Basil E. Frankweiler by E.L. Konigsburg
The Little Prince by Antoine de Saint-Exupery
Mrs. Frisby and the Rats of NIMH by Robert C. O'Brien
Old Yeller by Fred Gipson
Paul Revere's Ride by Henry Wadsworth Longfellow
Sarah, Plain and Tall by Patricia Mac Lachlan

10-12 years old
Anne of Green Gables by L.M. Montgomery
Bound for Oregon by Jean Van Leeuwen
Johnny Tremain by Esther Forbes
The Legend of Sleepy Hollow by Washington Irving
Sign of the Beaver by Elizabeth George Speare

11 years and older
Dave at Night by Gail Carson Levine
Little Women by Louisa May Alcott

Appendix B
Award-winning Books

Several of the titles in this guide are award and honor books, as well as book list selections.

Boston Globe-Hornbook Award

1999—Honor Book, Nonfiction
William Shakespeare and the Globe by Aliki

1974—Winner, Illustration
Jambo Means Hello: Swahili Alphabet Book illustrated by Tom Feelings, text by Muriel Feelings

Caldecott Award

1999—Winner
Snowflake Bentley by Jacqueline Briggs Martin

1992—Honor Book
Tar Beach by Faith Ringgold

1976—Honor Book
Strega Nona by Tomie de Paola

1975—Honor Book
Jambo Means Hello: Swahili Alphabet Book illustrated by Tom Feelings, text by Muriel Feelings

1949—Honor Book
Blueberries for Sal by Robert McCloskey

1942—Winner
Make Way for Ducklings by Robert McCloskey

1940—Honor Book
Madeline by Louis Bemelmans

Coretta Scott King Award

1992
Tar Beach by Faith Ringgold

Jane Addams Book Award

2000—Winner
Through My Eyes by Ruby Bridges

1999—Honor Book
This Land is Your Land by Woody Guthrie, with a tribute by Pete Seeger

National Jewish Book Award

1952—Winner
All-of-a-Kind-Family by Sydney Taylor

New York Times Best Illustrated Children's Books of the Year

1993—Winner
The Bracelet by Yoshiko Uchida

Newbery Award

2000—Honor Book
26 Fairmount Avenue by Tomie dePaola

1986—Winner
Sarah, Plain and Tall by Patricia MacLachlan

1984—Honor Book
The Sign of the Beaver by Elizabeth George Speare

1982—Honor Book
Ramona Quimby, Age 8 by Beverly Cleary

1972—Winner
Mrs. Frisby and the Rats of NIMH by Robert C. O'Brien

1968—Winner
From the Mixed-Up Files of Mrs. Basil E. Frankweiler by E. L. Konigsburg

1957—Honor Book
Old Yeller by Fred Gipson

1936—Winner
Caddie Woodlawn by Carol Ryrie Brink

Orbis Pictus Award for Outstanding Nonfiction for Children

2000—Winner
Through My Eyes by Ruby Bridges

2000—Recommended Book
William Shakespeare and the Globe by Aliki

List Selections

Capitol Choices, 1999
Amelia and Eleanor Go for a Ride by Pam Muñoz Ryan
Dave at Night by Gail Carson Levine
Huckabuck Family and How They Raised Popcorn in Nebraska and Quit and Came Back by Carl Sandburg
Through My Eyes by Ruby Bridges
William Shakespeare and the Globe by Aliki

Capitol Choices, 1998
Beautiful Warrior: The Legend of the Nun's Kung Fu by Emily Arnold McCully
Loud Emily by Alexis O'Neill

Children's Literature Choice List, 2000
Amelia and Eleanor Go for a Ride by Pam Munoz Ryan
Through My Eyes by Ruby Bridges
William Shakespeare and the Globe by Aliki

Children's Literature Choice List, 1999
Beautiful Warrior: The Legend of the Nun's Kung Fu by Emily Arnold McCully
Loud Emily by Alexis O'Neill

Appendix C
United States and World Maps

United States Map

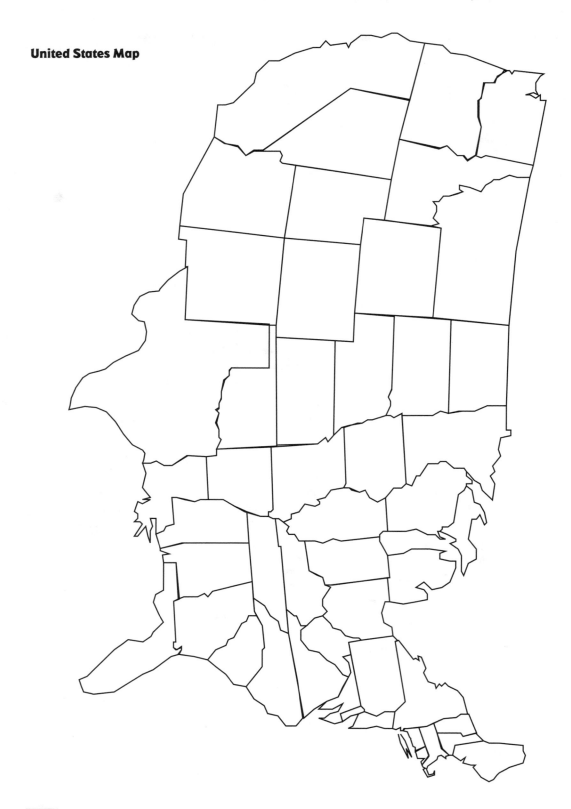

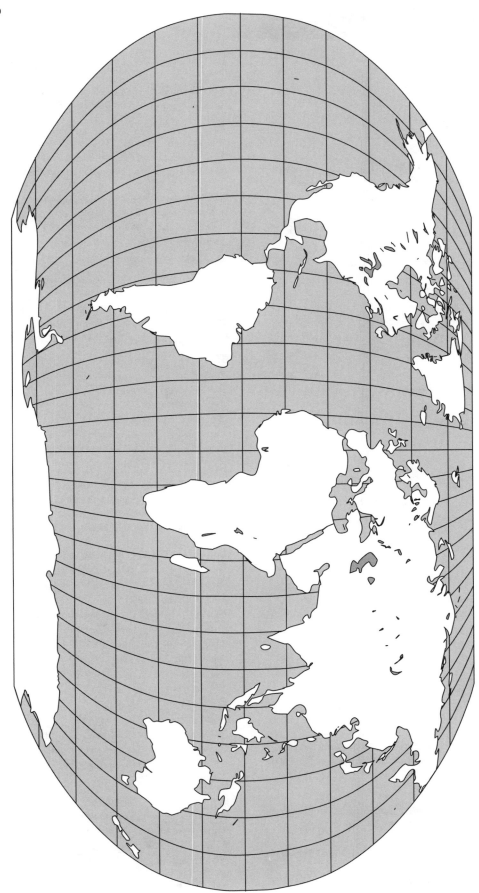

Author Index

Location Index

The books in this guide often take place in multiple settings within the United States and around the world. The titles are listed here under each of their locations.

Title Index